Strategic Wealth

A TACTICAL AND PRACTICAL GUIDE
TO WINNING IN RETIREMENT

TIM SULLIVAN

This book discusses general concepts for retirement planning, and is not intended to provide tax or legal advice. Individuals are urged to consult with their tax and legal professionals regarding these issues. This handbook should ensure that clients understand a) that annuities and some of their features have costs associated with them; b) that income received from annuities is taxable; and c) that annuities used to fund IRAs do not afford any additional measure of tax deferral for the IRA owner.

Copyright © 2017 by Gradient Positioning Systems (GPS). All rights reserved. No part of this publication may be reproduced, distributed, or transmitted in any form or by any means, electronic or mechanical, including photocopying, recording, or by any information storage and retrieval system, without written permission of the publisher, except in the case of brief quotations embodied in critical reviews and certain other noncommercial uses permitted by copyright law.

Gradient Positioning Systems, LLC and Timothy Sullivan are not affiliated with or endorsed by the Social Security Administration or any government agency.

Printed in the United States of America

First Printing, 2017

Gradient Positioning Systems, LLC
4105 Lexington Avenue North, Suite 110
Arden Hills, MN 55126
(877) 901-0894

TABLE OF CONTENTS

ACKNOWLEDGMENTS 1

INTRODUCTION 3

CHAPTER 1: HOW MUCH IS ENOUGH? 15

CHAPTER 2: RISK AND THE COLOR OF MONEY 31

CHAPTER 3: THE BUILDING BLOCKS OF
YOUR INCOME PLAN 43

CHAPTER 4: GOVERNMENT SERVICE AND SAVING 47

CHAPTER 5: MAKING SENSE OF SOCIAL SECURITY 67

CHAPTER 6: WHEN SOCIAL SECURITY ISN'T ENOUGH 85

CHAPTER 7: WHAT ARE YOUR OPTIONS FOR GROWTH? ... 105

CHAPTER 8: AVOIDING EMOTIONAL INVESTING 109

CHAPTER 9: THE MEANING OF YELLOW MONEY 115

CHAPTER 10: UNDERSTANDING NEW IDEAS
FOR INVESTING 131

CHAPTER 11: PAYING TAXES AS A RETIREE 135

CHAPTER 12: LOOKING INTO YOUR TAX FUTURE 147

CHAPTER 13: THE ROTH IRA AND TAX PLANNING 163

CHAPTER 14: WHAT KIND OF LEGACY WILL YOU LEAVE? ... 171

CHAPTER 15: PLANNING A SUCCESSFUL LEGACY 179

CHAPTER 16: FINDING THE RIGHT INVESTMENT ADVISOR ... 193

GLOSSARY 211

ACKNOWLEDGMENTS

Over the years, I have had the pleasure of working with and learning from some of the finest advisors in this industry. Each and every time that I meet with one of them, I try to come away with at least one new idea that I can incorporate into my practice to better my clients. These people have shaped and molded me into the advisor that I am today. I believe that you must always be trying to improve and advance yourself in life and in business. Saying this, I have to thank some special people in my life.

My wife Julie! You are simply an unbelievable woman and an inspiration to everyone who knows you! You're beautiful from the tips of your toes to the depths of your soul. Your smile lights up the room, your positive attitude is infectious, and your heart is ever so caring. Thank you for being an amazing wife and my best friend. You inspire me every day to live life to the fullest.

Being a parent isn't always easy but it is definitely rewarding and it's my greatest accomplishment in life. I want to thank my wonderful kids for giving me my best reasons to get up each and every morning. Devin, Kaitlynn, and Daylana you are truly amazing kids in your own different ways. I am very blessed to have been able to watch you grow up and find your way through life. Do not ever settle for anything less than you deserve. Your life, your goals and your dreams are there for you to accomplish.

Mom and Dad, thank you for giving me my work ethic and my drive. I learned from both of you that I can attain anything in life by just working hard and never giving up. More than anything though, you have taught me that family is everything. I am the father that I am today because of you. I love both of you!

My sisters, Michelle, Jen, Amanda and Joyce ... thank you! Thank you for always being there for me whenever I needed you. I love all of you very much and appreciate all that you have done for me over the years.

Finally, I must give a special thanks to the person that took me under his wings when I first got into this business that I love. Without him, I would not be writing this book. He has now become more than just a colleague of mine – I am proud to call him my dear friend. Bud Eastes, thank you for everything that you have ever done for me in my career, but most of all thank you for being a friend.

In loving memory of Aimee Sullivan.

INTRODUCTION

"A lot of what we ascribe to luck is not luck at all. It's seizing the day and accepting responsibility for your future."
– Howard Schultz

Retirement. It's what you've been working for all your life. Do you have a vision for what your retired life will look like? Do you have a plan that will ensure your vision comes to life? No matter who you are or how old you are, it's never too late to start that plan. If you're lucky, retirement will be a long, pleasant journey. If you plan well, you'll probably start to feel lucky, anyway.

PLAN TO BE LUCKY
When our parents and grandparents retired, things were very different. For one thing, the average life expectancy was shorter. Women born in 1915, for example, lived an average of 56.8

years, and men born in 1915 lived an average of 52.5 years. By 1946, the beginning of the Baby Boom, the average life expectancy for women was 69.4 and for men, 64.4.*

Today, if you live to age 65, you've got quite a retirement ahead of you. According to the Social Security Administration, on average, women who reach age 65 today can expect to live 21 more years (age 86.6), and men who reach age 65 can expect to live 19 more years (age 84.3).** That's a lot of years to live with no retirement plan, and Americans are feeling the strain. More than half of Americans worry that they will not have enough money to retire.***

Fortunately, there is a way to enjoy your retirement without worry. It requires making a plan. A plan is more important than ever before, not only because retirements are lasting longer than ever, but also because leveraging your assets to create income has become more complicated. Unlike past generations who were likely to work for the same company their entire lives and then retire with a pension, today most of us are responsible for our own retirements. We spend our careers budgeting and saving, putting away as much as we can in our 401(k)s and IRAs, and paying down debts. The scary thing, though, is that even the healthiest of retirement savings can be decimated by market volatility and lack of planning.

People do not plan to fail, but we do fail to plan!

Retirement today is a long journey, and it ought to be a happy one. Whatever road you'd like to follow during your retirement years, you first need two things: a guide and a map.

---

* http://demog.berkeley.edu/~andrew/1918/figure2.html
** http://www.ssa.gov/planners/lifeexpectancy.html
*** http://www.gallup.com/poll/168626/retirement-remains-americans-top-financial-worry.aspx

INTRODUCTION

WHAT KIND OF GUIDE DO I NEED?

One of the stressful things about retirement, and about life in general, is that we only get to do it once. The great thing about retirement, however, is that you can rely on a trusted guide. A financial professional who has helped hundreds of other retirees plan their successful journeys can also help you. How do you know if you have the right guide?

> » *I invited Bob and Alice into my office for their first meeting, and before they had even sat down, they began telling me about their distrust of financial advisors. They had stories to support their distrust, too: they had been lied to and taken advantage of on numerous occasions. No one, for example, had ever gone into the fine print with them, and they always got burned in the end. They knew now that they were looking for someone who would explain the fine print and help them understand their investments, but they weren't clear on what else they should be looking for. As a result, their retirement plan was in danger, and they were worried and scared.*
>
> *During that meeting, I told them about fiduciary responsibility, and I explained that an advisor held to that kind of standard is legally obligated to make recommendations in their clients' best interests.*
>
> *We decided to get started. I asked them to bring their tax return, all of their statements, their budget, life insurance policies, a mortgage statement, car insurance, etc. As they took out their paperwork, Alice asked me what it was all for. "No one has ever asked for any of these documents before." I could tell they were suspicious, and for good reason. They had trusted financial professionals before, and that trust had been violated. Now here I was, asking to dig deeper into their financial papers. Finding the right financial advisor can be a nerve-racking task.*

I explained my reasoning. "Without seeing your entire financial picture, I can't give you a second opinion that's true and accurate. There's no rush, however. Let's take this slowly and get to know each other. That way I can get a complete idea of your financial picture, and you can both decide if you like and trust me enough to work with me."

Over the next month, we had four meetings. By taking my time, I was able to build trust with Bob and Alice and earn their respect. I uncovered that their insurance policies were about to lapse, an event their agent never explained to them or warned them about. Any time you lose money, it's important, but Bob and Alice were relying on these policies to provide a legacy to their children. Sadly, they had paid premiums on these policies for many years and were distraught to find out that their children were not going to get anything if and when they lapsed. All was not lost, though. Because we caught it in time, I was able to use the remaining cash value along with some money that they had in CDs to get them the guaranteed death benefit they were looking for in the first place.

Armed with a better understanding of their retirement and income goals, I was also able to develop a retirement plan that showed Bob and Alice exactly how much income they should be able to pull from their investments when they stopped working. Because planning for every contingency is a crucial part of a successful retirement plan, we also looked at what would happen if one of them should pass away. What we discovered was a potential income problem if Bob passed away: Alice would lose a significant amount of income, including Bob's pension and one of their Social Security checks. Fortunately, I was able to create a guaranteed income plan for Alice that solved this potential problem in the future.

Next, it was time to focus on their investments. I worked with Bob and Alice to discover their risk tolerance. We dis-

INTRODUCTION

covered that their risk tolerance was not accurately reflected in their current portfolio. Not only were they not properly diversified, they also had several stocks and mutual funds that had under-performed over the last several years. I created customized reports, which demonstrated clearly that their investments were not allocated accordingly to their risk tolerance. With some reallocation, we were able to create a portfolio that fit both their risk tolerance and financial goals. Bob and Alice finally received the peace of mind they had been looking for.

Bob and Alice's story has a lot of steps, but one bottom line: they had met with a lot of financial professionals who insisted they had the answers for them without knowing what their financial goals were. After four meetings with me, we had begun to know each other well. I was in a good position to make recommendations that would address their goals and concerns. It's frustrating when I meet clients who've had to endure some negative experiences before finding an advisor who is prepared to take care of their retirement planning. It is one of the motivating forces behind this book: to help retirees and soon-to-be retirees find the right advisor and be prepared to create a plan that achieves their retirement dreams.

The first step in finding the right advisor is knowing what kind of advisors are out there. Take a look at the list below:

Insurance Agent
- Represents an affiliated insurance carrier, works only on behalf of their affiliated insurance carrier
- Held to suitability standards, not fiduciary standards
- Often call themselves "advisors"
- Limited *only* to insurance products
- Cannot give securities advice

Registered Representative (Broker)
- Represents an affiliated brokerage firm, works only on behalf of their affiliated firm
- Held to suitability standards, not fiduciary standards
- Registered representatives are typically an employee/contractor of a brokerage firm
- Typically compensated by commissions on product transactions
- Appears to be like an advisor in marketing materials and website presence

Registered Investment Advisor
- Represents their clients, works solely on behalf of their clients in a fiduciary capacity
- Offers comprehensive financial planning services
- Regulated by the SEC or states (as applicable)
- Fiduciary: legally required to put clients' interests first (a higher standard than suitability)
- Typically fee-based compensation for advice

These are just three of the many kinds of advisors out there, but it's enough to bring three main points of differentiation out:

1. Who does the advisor work for? If your advisor is not independent, that advisor works for a company or a brand, not for you. An advisor who represents a company can only offer the best possible solutions from that company, which is not the same thing as the *best possible solutions for you.*

2. What kind of standard is that advisor held to? Registered Investment Advisors are the only group of these three that are held to a fiduciary standard. This is an important distinction. Legally, an advisor who is held to a fiduciary standard is obligated to offer you advice that is solely in your best interest. They take into account your entire situation in order to determine what those best interests might be. On the other hand, advisors held to a suitability standard are only obligated to offer you a solution that is merely suitable. For example, flip flops are suitable footwear, but not if you're planning to move to Alaska. Your advisor needs to know your entire situation and goals in order to make the best recommendations, and you need the peace of mind that your advisor is held to a fiduciary standard. This is the rest of your life we're talking about, after all. You don't want to hang your hopes on someone who'd sell you flip-flops just because that was the product that paid the highest commission.

3. **How does the advisor get paid?** Speaking of commission, compensation is another crucial question. Advisors who receive fee-based compensation don't face the potential conflict of interest that commission-based or transaction-based professionals might encounter. This is not to say that those professionals are doing anything wrong; it's simply a matter of focus. As a retiree, you want and need a financial professional who is focused entirely on you, your goals and your future.

ABOUT STRATEGIC WEALTH ADVISORS GROUP, INC.

I founded Strategic Wealth Advisors Group, Inc. to help my clients achieve their financial peace of mind. I wanted to be able to build long-term relationships with my clients by solving their needs and helping them live out their retirement dreams. I found that the only way I could achieve this was to be independent and start my own company. This way I can offer my clients truly unbiased opinions. Independence also allows me to have access to unlimited options for my clients when it comes to insurance companies or Money Managers. I also strive to be known as a referable advisor, and I'm proud to say that the majority of my business comes from people my clients recommend me to. We are a full-service, comprehensive financial planning company. We offer both insurance products and active asset management. We serve clients in Ohio, Michigan, Pennsylvania, and Indiana. Our home office is located in Shelby Township, Michigan. We work with pre-retirees on growing their accumulated wealth, and with current retirees on making sure they have enough income throughout their retired years. We take pride in working with an aging American population and making sure that their investments are aligned with their goals. We offer safety and security during the time they will need to access their money the most.

Not only is it important to make sure you have proper help while accumulating your wealth, it is equally important to preserve what you have when you retire and work with someone who is going to be there for your children/beneficiaries to help in the distribution of your wealth upon your passing. We make sure there is a plan in place to transfer your wealth to your loved ones in the most beneficial way possible.

Impeccable customer service is essential to what we do. In addition to our ongoing educational seminars, we provide complimentary, one-on-one meetings in our office or in the privacy of your home. We know that as our clients age, they might not be able to make it into our office. It has always been our standard practice to make ourselves available to meet our clients at their convenience in the comfort of their homes if they prefer. We would love to meet with you too, and give you the financial checkup you deserve.

Years ago, I learned how precious life really is. Each new day is not promised! That's why we need to spend our retirement years enjoying life and living it to its fullest. In order to do that though, we need to have our financial affairs in order, we have to know that our investments will provide the retirement income that we want and need, and that our nest egg is always protected.

While sitting in my office 14 years ago, I received a call from my wife. Her doctor had just informed her she had breast cancer. As you can imagine, this turned our world upside down. This showed me that there's no guarantee in life. You can have all of the money in the world, but without your health, it means absolutely nothing. During the past 14 years, my wife has gone through numerous chemo and radiation treatments. We have changed doctors and hospitals several times during this time for all different reasons.

This experience has taught me to be a much better advisor. It has taught me to be a well-rounded comprehensive advisor. It's not just about the highest return (that doesn't mean that we do not want to earn a good return). It is about making sure that our "rainy day" situations are taken care of. Your "rainy day" could be similar to my wife's, it could be necessary to enter a nursing home, or it might be making sure that all of your worst-case-scenario fears are covered. That is why we have car and home insurance, right? If we were to get into an auto accident or if our house were to catch on fire, our insurance will replace these things. What protection do we have if and when the market goes down? What if on the day that we need to take money out of our retirement nest egg to help us through a "rainy day" situation, the market takes a major hit? How will this affect our retirement nest egg? Why do we risk our retirement nest egg so much and not make sure that it is better protected?

This brings me back to my wife's situation: we learned that we have some control when it comes to the treatment of her cancer. We make the decision on what treatment she will receive and what doctor she will be treated by. Similarly, you are in control of your retirement assets. You owe it to yourself to get a second opinion to make sure that your investments are in line with your risk tolerance. If your advisor isn't talking to you on a quarterly basis, not talking to you about Social Security benefits, income planning, principal protection, long-term care, etc., then you really need to stop and ask yourself: "Why am I doing business with him/her?" This is your money and you only have one life. You need to take control of it and make sure you find an advisor that will work for you and provide you with the service you deserve. Just like we fired and hired new doctors, you can do the same with your advisor. Remember, you only have one life. Live it to its fullest!

OUR PROCESS

You and your family are at the center of our process. Strategic Wealth Advisors Group, Inc. helps you and your family see where you are today, where you would like to be financially, and what it will take to get there.

We use a structured financial planning process to bring you clarity, confidence and financial peace of mind. This process focuses on:

1. **An Emotional Check-In:** A series of questions that will help you identify where you are emotionally in relation to your finances and investments.
2. **A Financial Check-In:** We'll help you take a financial inventory, looking at your assets, debts, insurance coverage, and estate documents. The inventory brings you further clarity, and it helps Strategic Wealth Advisors Group, Inc. planners make more educated and appropriate recommendations for you and your family.
3. **Where Are You Trying To Go?** This stage of the planning process is about vision and goal setting. You'll identify what you want financially, then we put a price tag on your financial goals. You and your family have the opportunity to articulate and prioritize your financial goals so you can achieve them.

4. **What Will It Take To Get There?** This is an action step, in which we establish a plan and implement it so you achieve your financial goals. We take pride in keeping things simple and explaining this process in a way you can understand. Unlike other advisors, when you leave our office, you will be able to understand and make sense of the strategy employed to accomplish your goals.

Our goal is to build mutual trust and respect through a series of meetings and steps, all of which allow us to get a better sense of your goals and concerns. We take each new client through four strategy sessions:

1st Strategy Session:
- Discuss your goals and concerns
- Review your confidential financial outline
- Review all your assets so we can prepare an analysis

2nd Strategy Session:
- Present *your* Personalized Retirement Plan
- Focus on IRAs
- Review Multi-Generational IRA Report
- Recommendations on Lifetime Income Planning (Reports)
- Rule of 100 report (Red Money & Green Money)
- Meet with our estate planning attorney

3rd Strategy Session:
Start implementing your retirement plan
- Focus is on Non-Qualified Accounts (Securities)
- Discuss life insurance and long-term care solutions
- Meet with our mortgage loan originator (if needed)

4th Strategy Session:
Continue implementing your retirement plan
- Focus on reducing taxes
- 2nd Opinion tax review
- Roth IRA conversion report
- Funeral planning (Funeral Trust)
- Meet with our property and casualty agent

I believe the number one risk that we need to eliminate for a client heading into retirement is longevity risk. Longevity risk is a risk multiplier! The longer we live (longevity risk), the more likely that we will experience market risk, sequence of returns risk, withdrawal rate risk, inflation risk and deflation risk. Therefore, we need to eliminate longevity risk out of our clients' portfolios in order for them to live a long and happy retirement.

When I began my career in estate planning, I quickly began to see how many retirees were in need of better financial planning. As the founder and CEO of Strategic Wealth Advisors Group, Inc., I lead a team of experts that helps individuals and families achieve financial peace of mind. Retirement should be everything you've worked for and everything you've dreamed of, but that will only happen if you have a strategic plan in place and a guide to help you achieve every goal along the way.

– *Timothy Sullivan*
Strategic Wealth Advisory Group, Inc.

1
HOW MUCH IS ENOUGH?

"Good fortune is what happens when opportunity meets with planning."
– Thomas Edison

There is no such thing as a one-size-fits-all retirement plan. You will read a different story every day in the news telling you that you need 80 percent of your current income, or 130 percent, or maybe even 65 percent. No one, however, can tell you what amount of money will allow you to have a peaceful, secure retirement without knowing *you*. That's something I learned from Maxine.

» *Maxine was 65 years old when she first came into my office. Maxine was single and had no kids. For 35 years, she had* *worked at a local diner, where she baked pies. Maxine had all of her paperwork in order when she arrived for our first meeting, and she showed me her most recent IRA statement. Her account balance was $785,000.*

"Maxine," I said. "This is a great start, especially given the fact that you're only 65. Are you hoping to finally retire? Maxine shook her head. "That's not for me. That's for my niece and nephew." Then Maxine told me the thing that was the most amazing: she didn't plan on retiring. Ever. And she didn't. Maxine knew two things: she had a twin sister who was her polar opposite, financially speaking, and that sister had two kids, Maxine's beloved niece and nephew. Maxine worked until she was age 74, when she had a stroke. Always the planner, Maxine had invested in long-term care insurance, which paid for her last, and only, month of nursing home care. When she passed away, her estate, as we planned, went to her sister, niece and nephew.

Maxine never planned on retiring, but she did have a plan for exactly what she wanted her savings to do.

Laurel was Maxine's sister. Laurel and her husband Dave both retired at age 62 and took their Social Security benefits immediately. I never knew how much they had saved for retirement, but I do know that by the time Maxine's money came through, both of them had gone back to work part-time. It was generosity that got Laurel into trouble, Maxine told me many times. If anyone ever needed help, Laurel helped. Laurel bought extravagant birthday and Christmas gifts, as well.

"Once she even bought me a cruise!" Maxine had laughed. "Imagine that! Me, on a cruise." She had thanked her sister and asked her to refund the gift. She worried about her sister and who would take care of her. As a result, Maxine had worked with me and our firm's strategic legal partner to leave

> *instructions that her IRA be divided into thirds and used to purchase annuities with income riders. Maxine wanted to be sure, above all, that her sister and her sister's kids would have reliable incomes. When the sad day came and Maxine passed away, I met with Laurel and her kids and gave them the news. After we discussed all of the next steps and signed all the papers, I was headed to the door when Laurel took me aside. She said she had always wished her sister would enjoy life more and save less, but now, she wanted to be sure that she made the most of her sister's unbelievable gift. She asked if I might help them get their affairs in order, too.*

Do you have enough money to retire? If you're like Maxine or Laurel, the answer is probably no. Maxine was so focused on saving for her family that she would never be satisfied with "enough," and her sister, Laurel, was way on the other end of the spectrum: she retired with no plan at all and had to go back to work.

The good news is that you're probably not like Maxine or Laurel. You're probably like most people, somewhere in the middle. You've worked and saved, and you've got a 401(k) or an IRA (or several). You know you've got Social Security benefits coming, but you're not sure how much that will be. In fact, you're not quite sure how all of your different assets will come together to create income for the next 20 plus years, or how much income you can generate. If that sounds like you, don't worry. You're not alone. You're in the same place as many soon-to-be retirees, and you're in the perfect place to start creating your own customized, strategic retirement plan.

As you enter retirement, you're not just transitioning into a whole new kind of living; you're also moving into an entirely new financial phase of your life. Up until the moment you retire, you're in the **Accumulation Phase**, the time in your life when you accumulate assets. You work. You save as much as you can.

You invest. During this period, you sock away everything you can, like a squirrel preparing for winter. On the day you retire and give up that paycheck, though, you're entering a new phase that we call the **Distribution Phase**. During this phase, you're no longer earning an income, and it's time for all of those assets to start creating an income for you.

There once was a time when people left all of their assets in the market, drawing a percentage out every month or year to live on and pay their bills. As we'll discuss in "New Ideas for Retirement," however, the stock market has become increasingly volatile. The recent economic downturns of 2001 and 2008 have shown us that putting all of your life's savings in the market might not be the best recipe for a peaceful, worry-free retirement.

As you begin to plan your retirement, you might consider an alternate option: a distribution plan that structures your assets to create guaranteed income first and plan for growth second. Your ideal retirement has two parts:
- Assets structured to create guaranteed income
- Assets structured for growth

In addition to those objectives, your plan also needs to take into account all of the other complex factors that can affect a retiree's income. Some of these things include required minimum distributions (RMDs), taxes and your goals for your legacy. All of theses things can have an enormous impact on your retirement, and they need to be considered in your plan.

Now that you know there's more to saving and planning for retirement than filing for your Social Security benefit and drawing income from your 401(k), you can begin to **create a strategy for your retirement** that can have a significant impact on your financial landscape after you stop drawing a paycheck. Understanding how to manage your assets entails risk management, risk diversification, tax planning and income planning preparation throughout your life stages. These strategies can help you leverage more from each one of the hard-earned dollars you set aside for your retirement.

Some people file for Social Security on day one of their retirement. Others rely on supplemental income from an IRA or another retirement account. Working with a financial professional can help you determine your best course of action.

NEW IDEAS FOR RETIREMENT

Advice about what to do with money has been around as long as money has existed. Hindsight allows us to see which advice was good and which advice didn't cut the mustard. Some sources of advice have been around for a very long time. While there are some basic investment concepts that have stood the test of time, most strategies that work adapt to changing conditions in the market, in the economy and the world, as well as changes in your personal circumstances.

The reality is that investment strategies and savings plans that worked in the past have encountered challenging new circumstances that have turned them on their heads. The Great Recession of the early 2000s highlighted how old investment ideas were not only ineffective but incredibly destructive to the retirement plans of millions of Americans. The dawn of an entirely restructured health care system brings with it new options and challenges that will undoubtedly change the way insurance companies provide investment solutions and services.

Perhaps the most important lessons investors learned from the Great Recession is that not understanding where your money is invested (and the potential risks of those investments) can work against you, your plans for retirement and your legacy. Saving and investing money isn't enough to truly get the most out of it. You must have a planful approach to managing your assets.

Essentially, managing your money and your investments is an ongoing process that requires customization and adaptation to a changing world. And make no mistake; the world is always changing. What worked for your parents or even your parents' parents was probably good advice back then. People in retirement or approaching retirement today need new ideas and professional guidance.

HOPE SO VS. KNOW SO MONEY

Let's take a look at some of the basic truths about money as it relates to saving for retirement.

There are essentially two kinds of money: *Hope So* and *Know So*.

"Know So" Money	"Hope So" Money
Offers a minimum guarantee* but may pose risks other than market risk	*This money can go up or down in value*
Safer Instruments	**At-Risk Instruments**
Checking-Savings-CDs**	*Stocks-Bonds*
Treasuries	*Variable Annuities*
Money Market	*Mutual Funds*
Fixed Annuities	*REITs*

---

*Guaranteed investments refer to a checking account, savings account, certificate of deposit or fixed annuity. For a fixed annuity, guarantee is based on the claims paying ability of issuing insurance carrier and the IRS may impose a 10 percent penalty on withdrawals prior to age 59½.

** Investors should understand when the CD matures, how often it pays interest and how much interest it pays. Find out if the issuer has the right to call or redeem the CD prior to maturity. Compare the yields quoted versus those of non-callable alternatives. Understand secondary market liquidity in case it is necessary to cash out prior to maturity. Investors should check all their existing deposits at that bank prior to purchasing its CD so they won't exceed FDIC insurance limits. Finally, consider all risks and benefits and how this investment alternative may help meet investment objectives. Remember, brokered CDs may not be suitable for everyone.

Everyone can divide their money into these two categories. Some have more of one kind than the other. The goal isn't to eliminate one kind of money but to balance them as you approach retirement.

ORGANIZING YOUR ASSETS

Hope So Money is money that is at risk. It fluctuates with the market. It has no minimum guarantee. It is subject to investor activity, stock prices, market trends, buying trends, etc. You get the picture. This money is exposed to more risk but also has the potential for more reward. Because the market is subject to change, you can't really be sure what the value of your investments will be worth in the future. You can't really *rely* on it at all. For this reason, we refer to it as Hope So Money. This doesn't mean you shouldn't have some money invested in the market, but it would be dangerous to assume you can know what it will be worth in the future.

Hope So Money is an important element of a retirement plan, especially in the early stages of planning when you can trade volatility for potential returns, and when a longer investment timeframe is available to you. In the long run, time can smooth out the ups and downs of money exposed to the market. Working with a professional and leveraging a long-term investment strategy has the potential to create rewarding returns from Hope So Money.

Know So Money, on the other hand, is safer when compared to Hope So Money. Know So Money is made up of dependable, low-risk or no-risk money, and investments that you can count on. Social Security is one of the most common forms of Know So Money. Income you draw or will draw from Social Security is guaranteed. You have paid into Social Security your entire career, and you can rely on that money during your retirement. Unlike the market, rates of growth for Know So Money are dependent on 10-year treasury rates. The 10-year treasury, or TNX, is commonly considered to represent a very secure and safe place for your money, hence Know So Money. The 10-year treasury drives key rates for things such as mortgage rates or CD rates. Know So Money may not be as exciting as Hope So Money, but it is safer. You can safely be fairly sure you will have it in the future.

Knowing the difference between Hope So and Know So Money is an important step towards a successful retirement plan. People who are 55 or older and who are looking ahead to retirement should be relying on more Know So Money than Hope So Money.

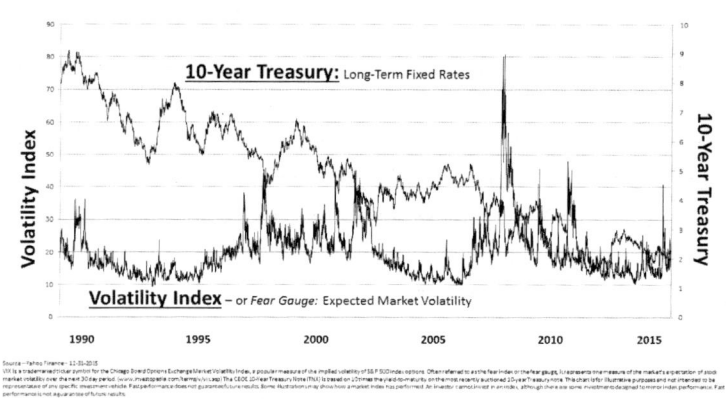

The VIX, or volatility index, of the market represents expected market volatility. When the VIX Drops, economic experts expect less volatility. When the VIX rises, more volatility is expected.

1. *VIX is a trademarked ticker symbol for the Chicago Board Options Exchange (CBOE) Market Volatility Index, a popular measure of the implied volatility of S&P 500 index options. Often referred to as the fear index or the fear gauge, it represents one measure of the market's expectation of stock market volatility over the next 30 day period. (wikipedia.com)*
2. *The CBOE 10-Year Treasury note (TNX) is based on 10 times the yield-to-maturity on the most recently auctioned 10-year Treasury note.*

Ideally, the rates of return on Hope So and Know So Money would have an overlapping area that provided an acceptable rate of risk for both types of money. In the early 1990s, interest rates were high and market volatility was low. At that time, you could invest in either Hope So or Know So Money options because the rates of return were similar from both Know So and Hope So investments, and you were likely to be fairly successful with a wide range of investment options. At that time, you could expose yourself to an acceptable amount of risk or an acceptable fixed rate. Basically, it was difficult to make a mistake during that time period. Today, you don't have those options. Market volatility is at all-time highs while interest rates are at all-time lows. They are so far apart from each other that it is hard to know what to do with your money.

Yesterday's investment rules may not work today. Not only could they hamper achieving your goals, they may actually harm your financial situation. We are currently in a period when the rates for Know So Money options are at historic lows, and the volatility of Hope So Money is higher than ever. There is no overlapping acceptable rate, making both options less than ideal. *Because of this uncertain financial landscape, wise investment strategies are more important now than ever.*

This unique situation requires fresh ideas and investment tools that haven't been relied on in the past. Investing the way your parents did will not pay off. The majority of investment ideas used by financial professionals in the 1990s aren't applicable to today's markets. That kind of investing will likely get you in trouble and compromise your retirement. Today, you need a better PLAN.

HOW MUCH RISK ARE YOU EXPOSED TO?

Many investors don't know how much risk they are exposed to. It is helpful to organize your assets so you can have a clear understanding of how much of your money is at risk and how much is in safer holdings. This process starts with listing all your assets. Let's take a look at the two kinds of money:

Hope So Money is, as the name indicates, money that you *hope* will be there when you need it. Hope So Money represents what you would like to get out of your investments. Examples of Hope So Money include:
- Stock market funds, including index funds
- Mutual funds
- Variable annuities
- REITS

Know So Money is money that you know you can count on. It is safer money that isn't exposed to the level of volatility as the asset types noted above. You can more confidently count on having this money when you need it. Examples of Know So Money are:
- Government backed bonds
- Savings and checking accounts
- Fixed income annuities
- CDs
- Treasuries
- Money market accounts

> » Ben had a modest brokerage account that he added to when he could. When he changed jobs a couple years ago, at age 58, Ben transferred his 401(k) assets into an IRA. Just a few years from retirement, he is now beginning to realize that nearly every dollar he has saved for retirement is subject to market risk.
>
> Intuitively, he knows that the time has come to shift some assets to an alternative that is safer, but how much is the right amount?

RULE OF 100

Determining the amount of risk that is right for you is dependent on a number of variables. You need to feel comfortable with where and how you are investing your money, and your financial professional is obligated to help you make decisions that put your money in places that fit your risk criteria.

Your retirement needs to first accommodate your day-to-day income needs. How much money do you need to maintain your lifestyle? When do you need it?

Managing your risk by having a balance of Hope So Money vs. Know So Money is a good start that will put you ahead of the curve. But how much Know So Money is enough to secure your income needs during retirement, and how much Hope So Money is enough to allow you to continue to benefit from an improving market?

In short, how do you begin to know how much risk you should be exposed to?

While there is no single approach to investment risk determination advice that is universally applicable to everyone, there are some helpful guidelines. One of the most useful is called *The Rule of 100*.

The average investor needs to accumulate assets to create a retirement plan that provides income during retirement and also allows for legacy planning. To accomplish this, they need to balance the amount of risk to which they are exposed. Risk is required because, while Know So Money is safer, more reliable and more dependable, it doesn't grow very fast, if at all. Today's historically low interest rates barely break even with current inflation. Hope So Money, while less dependable, has more potential for growth. Hope So Money can eventually become Know So Money once you move it to an investment with lower risk. Everyone's risk diversification will be different depending on their goals, age and their existing assets.

So how do you decide how much risk your assets should be exposed to? Where do you begin? Luckily, there's a guideline you can use to start making decisions about risk management. It's called the Rule of 100.

THE RULE OF 100

The Rule of 100 is a general rule that helps shape asset diversification* for the average investor. The rule states that the number 100 minus an investor's age equals the amount of assets they should have exposed to risk.

The Rule of 100: 100 − (your age) = the percentage of your assets that should be exposed to risk (Hope So Money)

For example, if you are a 30-year-old investor, the Rule of 100 would indicate that you should be focusing on investing primarily in the market and taking on a substantial amount of risk in your portfolio. The Rule of 100 suggests that 70 percent of your investments should be exposed to risk.

100 − (30 years of age) = 70 percent

Now, not every 30-year-old should have exactly 70 percent of their assets in mutual funds and stocks. The Rule of 100 is based on your chronological age, not your "financial age," which could vary based on your investment experience, your aversion or acceptance of risk and other factors. While this rule isn't an ironclad solution to anyone's finances, it's a pretty good place to start. Once you've taken the time to look at your assets with a professional to deter-

---

Diversification and asset allocation does not assure or guarantee better performance and cannot eliminate the risk of investment loss, fluctuating prices, and uncertain returns. Before investing, you should carefully read the applicable volatility disclosure for each of the underlying funds, which can be found in the current prospectus.

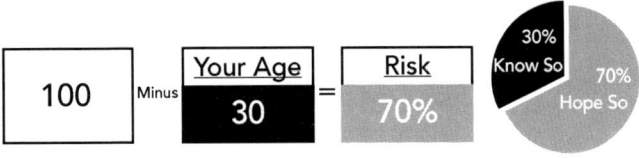

mine your risk exposure, you can use the Rule of 100 to make changes that put you in a more stable investment position—one that reflects your comfort level.

Perhaps when you were age 30 and starting your career, like in the example above, it made sense to have 70 percent of your money in the market: you had time on your side. You had plenty of time to save more money, work more and recover from a downturn in the market. Retirement was ages away, and your earning power was increasing. And indeed, younger investors should take on more risk for exactly those reasons. The potential reward of long-term involvement in the market outweighs the risk of investing when you are young.

Risk tolerance generally reduces as you get older, however. If you are 40 years old and lose 30 percent of your portfolio in a market downturn this year, you have 20 or 30 years to recover it. If you are 68 years old, you have five to 10 years (or less) to make the same recovery. That new circumstance changes your whole retirement perspective. At age 68, it's likely that you simply aren't as interested in suffering through a tough stock market. There is less time to recover from downturns, and the stakes are higher. The money you have saved is money you will soon need to provide you with income, or is money that you already need to meet your income demands.

Much of the flexibility that comes with investing earlier in life is related to *compounding*. Compounded earnings can be incredibly powerful over time. The longer your money has time to compound, the greater your wealth will be. This is what most people talk about when they refer to putting their money to work. This is also why the Rule of 100 favors risk for the young. If you start investing when you are young, you can invest smaller amounts of money in a more aggressive fashion because you have the potential to make a profit in a rising market and you can harness the power of compounding earnings. When you are 40, 50 or 60 years old, that potential becomes less and less and you are forced to have more money at lower amounts of risk to realize the same returns. **It basically becomes more expensive to prudently invest the older you get.**

You risk not having a recovery period the older you get, so should have less of your assets at risk in volatile investments. You should shift with the Rule of 100 to protect your assets and ensure that they will provide you with the income you need in retirement. Let's look at another example that illustrates how the Rule of 100 becomes more critical as you age. An 80-year-old investor who is retired and is relying on retirement assets for income, for example, needs to depend on a solid amount of Know So Money. The Rule of 100 says an 80-year-old investor should have a maximum of 20 percent of his or her assets at risk. Depending on the investor's financial position, even less risk exposure may be required. You are the only person who can make this kind of determination, but the Rule of 100 can help. Everyone has their own level of comfort. Your Rule of 100 results will be based on your values and attitudes as well as your comfort with risk.

The Rule of 100 can apply to overarching financial management and to specific investment solutions that you own as well. Take the 401(k) for example. Many people have them, but not many people understand how their money is allocated within their 401(k). An employer may have someone who comes in once a year and explains the models and options that employees can choose from, but that's as much guidance as most 401(k) holders get. Many 401(k) options include target date funds that change their risk exposure over time, essentially following a form of the Rule of 100. Selecting one of these options can often be a good move for employees because they shift your risk as you age, securing more Know So Money when you need it.

A financial professional can look at your assets with you and discuss alternatives to optimize your balance between Know So and Hope So Money.

SET IT, BUT DON'T FORGET IT
The Rule of 100 reminds us that your financial goals and concerns can change as you age. Your life won't divide neatly into the Accumulation Phase and Distribution Phase. There are always little changes along the way. The world changes. Our kids grow up. Our kids have kids. Our health has good and not so great periods. As such, your financial plan will need adjustments as well. Even the most carefully crafted retirement plan will need to be adjusted regularly if it is to remain successful.

Take your legacy, for example. When you set up your IRA, you most likely filled out beneficiary paperwork. If you were single at the time, you might have named a sibling or a niece or nephew as your beneficiary. What if you got married, had children, or had grandchildren? The people you would like to name as beneficiaries might change several times over your lifetime, but if the paperwork doesn't change, your wishes won't be followed.

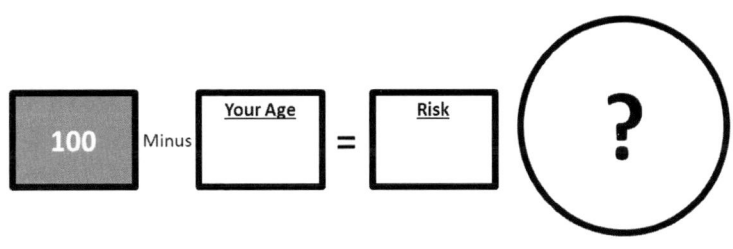

Other changes might take place during your retirement, as well. You might suddenly decide to start traveling the world, and that will require adjusting your assets. You might have a grandchild and decide to move some assets into an investment to save for college. The point is this: you should have the retirement you want, and that requires a living, changing retirement plan. That means you should choose a financial advisor you'll be happy to see at least once a year. Retirement plans aren't just a one-time thing. A good advisor will see you quarterly, bi-annually or annually to review your goals and adjust your plan as needed.

CHAPTER 1 RECAP //

- While you are working and saving, you are in the Accumulation Phase. On the day you retire and begin drawing an income from those assets, you enter the Distribution Phase.
- The volatility of the stock market in recent decades has led to new ideas for retirement planning that allow retirees to structure their assets for guaranteed income, and then think about growth options.
- There is money you hope you'll have in the future, and there's money you know you'll have in the future. Make sure you know how much you need when you retire.
- Organizing your assets starts with making a list. You can then understand how each asset is balanced for risk.
- Your exposure to risk is ultimately determined by you.
- Use the Rule of 100 as a general guiding principle when determining how much risk your retirement investments should be exposed to (100 − [your age] = [percentage of your investments that can comfortably exposed to risk]).
- Your retirement plan is not a "fix it and forget it" situation. Your goals and concerns will change during your retirement, and your plan needs to be reviewed at least on an annual basis to be sure it stays consistent with your goals.

2
RISK AND THE COLOR OF MONEY?

"The way to wealth, if you desire it, is as plain as the way to market. It depends chiefly on two words: industry and frugality. Waste neither time nor money, but make the best use of both."
– Benjamin Franklin

A number of years ago, a woman named Kathleen came to one of my seminars. By chance, she had come across an invitation for one of my seminars just a few weeks after her husband passed away, and a little voice told her that it was important for her to go. She wasn't sure why, but she decided to follow that advice.

After the seminar, Kathleen set up an appointment with me. She showed up with a box of files. During that appointment, I realized that she had a huge amount of accounts all over the place, including IRAs and Roth IRAs, some of which were in annuities, CDs, broker-

age accounts and her late husband's 401(k), as well as her own. She also had savings and checking accounts at four different banks. The family had moved several times for both her and her husband's jobs. Her accounts ran the gamut from tax-qualified to tax-advantaged, but she wasn't sure which was which. When I asked her why she had so many accounts, she said, "This was Thomas's thing, and I never worried about it. Now it drives me crazy. I have no idea what's what!"

We agreed that the first order of business, for her peace of mind, was to consolidate and simplify her financial life. She also told me that in her frenzy to try and manage all of these various accounts, she opened and read every statement, and it seemed like every time she opened one, it was losing money. It frightened her. That's why she had decided to make an appointment after the seminar. She hoped I could help her do away with the anxiety of all these unmanageable accounts as well as the fear that all of their life savings was slipping through the cracks.

"This has already been so hard," she explained. "I don't want to leave this big box of files for my kids to have to wade through if I pass away suddenly."

The first order of business was to figure out everything that Kathleen had and how much risk those assets faced. We talked about the Red Money, or high-risk, investments that were losing money, and Kathleen explained that after losing her husband, she wasn't comfortable with investments that had a high potential for loss. After some discussion, we decided to consolidate all of her non-qualified accounts into one account. After worrying over all the RMDs she needed to make, or might possibly miss, Kathleen was delighted to narrow it down to one. Plus, she explained, she wasn't even using the RMDs she drew, but rather depositing them back into one of her savings accounts. She and her husband had saved well, but they had always agreed that their goal was to leave as much as possible to their kids. They had three children, all of whom they wanted to support as much as possible. Their youngest son had disabilities that would require *special care for his entire life, a fact that Kathleen and Thomas had been planning for since he was born. We decided that rather than putting her RMDs into savings, where they were earning less than the rate of inflation, she could purchase a life insurance policy that would increase her legacy to her children by maximizing the amount she could leave to them. Not only would she be able to leave them more money but this would also provide them with a tax-free inheritance. With the assets left over, we set about making a plan that would ensure Kathleen enjoyed a happy retirement herself, knowing that her assets and her children were protected.*

Whether you already have a plan in place or you are starting from scratch, you want to be sure it's the right plan for you. The first thing you need to understand is what you have. Some of the most common mistakes retirees make are caused by not understanding exactly what assets they have, how those assets work and what risk those assets face. Like Kathleen in the story above, who didn't know what her assets were and why they kept losing money, this lack of clarity can cause a great deal of stress and risk the retirement and legacy goals you've worked so hard to earn.

You can't start building your retirement if you aren't sure what kinds of materials you're working with, so it's important to get very clear on what you own right now. After that, it becomes much easier to decide how you want to structure your assets to generate income and fund your retirement dreams.

To understand your current assets, it can be helpful to assign colors to the different kinds of money and their level of risk. For our purposes, Know So Money (which is safer and more dependable) is green. Hope So Money (which is exposed to risk and fluctuates with the market) is red. A financial professional can help you better understand the color of the money in your investment portfolio.

The fact of the matter is that a lot of people don't know their level of exposure to risk. Visually organizing your assets is an important and powerful way to get a clear picture of what kind of money you have, where it is and how you can best use it in the future. This process is as simple as listing your assets and assigning them a color based on their status as Know So or Hope So Money. Work with your financial professional to create a comprehensive inventory of your assets to understand what you are working with before making any decisions. This may be the first time you have ever sat down and sorted out all of your assets, allowing you to see how much money you have at risk in the market. Comparing the color of your investments will give you an idea of how near or far you are from adhering to the Rule of 100.

Green Money	Red Money
"Green Money" is safer.	"Red Money" is at risk.
This is money that offers a minimum guarantee but it may pose risks other than market risk.	This is money that can go up or down in value. It may pose risk if it is not properly managed to serve a specific purpose in a comprehensive plan.

Over the course of your lifetime, it is likely that you have acquired a variety of assets. Assets can range from money that you have in a savings account or a 401(k), to a pension or an IRA. You have earned money and have made financial decisions based on the best information you had at the time. When viewed as a whole, however, you might not have an overall strategy for the management of your assets. As we have seen, it's more important

RISK AND THE COLOR OF MONEY?

than ever to know which of your assets are at risk. High market volatility and low treasury rates make for challenging financial topography. Navigating this financial landscape starts with planful asset management that takes into account your specific needs and options.

Even if you feel that you have plenty of money in your 401(k) or IRA, not knowing how much *risk* those investments are exposed to can cause you major financial suffering. Take the market crash of 2008 for example. In 2008, the average investor lost 30 percent of their 401(k). If more people had shifted their investments away from risk as they neared retirement age (i.e. the Rule of 100), they may have lost a lot less money going into retirement.

When using the Rule of 100 to calculate your level of risk, your financial age might be different than your chronological age, however. The way you organize your assets depends on your goals and your level of comfort with risk. Whatever you determine the appropriate amount of risk for you to be, you will need to organize your portfolio to reflect your goals. If you have more Red Money than Green Money, in particular, you will need to make decisions about how to move it. You can work with a financial professional to find appropriate Green Money options for your situation.

The next step is to know the right amount and ratio of Green and Red Money for you at your stage of retirement planning.

Investing heavily in Red Money and gambling all of your assets on the market is incredibly risky no matter where you fall within the Rule of 100. Money in the market can't be depended on to generate income, and a plan that leans too heavily on Red Money can easily fail, especially when investment decisions are influenced by emotional reactions to market downturns and recoveries. Not only is this an unwise plan, it can be incredibly stressful to an investor who is gambling everything on stocks and mutual funds.

But a plan that uses too much Green Money avoids all volatility and can also fail.

» *Luke had most of his savings in variable annuities that were sustaining consistent losses, and he wanted to move that money. He wanted to meet with me to put together the best plan for this large portion of his nest egg that he was planning to move. By the time he came in for the appointment, though, just a week later, he had already made a move. He had withdrawn one of his variable annuities and moved it into a CD.*

"I got so worried about the loss they could suffer, even in just one week, that I decided to move one of them. I was lying awake at night worrying about what was happening to my savings, so I just did it."

The good news, in this case, was that because Luke's accounts had been performing poorly, he didn't trigger a huge tax event when he moved that money. The bad news, though, was that he had just moved this money into a CD that was earning less than 1 percent interest every year. It's true that they did come with principal protection. Technically, the balance would not decrease. But considering the destructive power of inflation, making your dollar today worth significantly less than your dollar in 10 or 20 years, the truth was that Luke's savings weren't really safe at all. His new challenge was inflation risk!

I explained the inflation risk he now faced, and showed him that he was paying roughly 4 percent per year in fees within his variable annuities. These fees added up to about $25,000 per year. In the end, we were able to mitigate his risk by re-positioning the rest of his variable annuities, and provide him with the principal protection that he was looking for, while still allowing him un-capped interest earning potential. Also, it wasn't too late for Luke to cancel his CD transaction. This allowed him to better invest this money and leverage it to provide him with more earning potential. After *it was all done, Luke said he was finally able to sleep at night again.*

Investing all of your money in Certificates of Deposit (CDs), savings accounts, money markets and other low return accounts may provide interest and income, but that likely won't be enough to keep pace with inflation. If you focus exclusively on income from Green Money and avoid owning any stocks or mutual funds in your portfolio, you won't be able to leverage the potential for long-term growth your portfolio needs to stay healthy and productive. This is where the Rule of 100 can help you determine how much of your money should be invested in the market to anticipate your future needs.

Green Money becomes much more important as you age. While you want to reduce the amount of Red Money you have and to transition it to Green Money, you don't necessarily need all of it to generate income for you right away. Taking a closer look at Green Money, you will see there are actually different types.

TYPES OF GREEN MONEY: *NEED NOW AND NEED LATER*

Money that you need to depend on for income is Green Money. Once you have filled the income gap at the beginning of your retirement, you may have money left over.

There are two types of Green Money: money used for income and money used for accumulation to meet your income needs in five, 10 or 20 years. Money needed for income is Need Now Money. It is money you need to meet your basic needs, to pay your bills, your mortgage if you have one and the costs associated with maintaining your lifestyle. Money used for accumulation is Need Later Money. It's money that you don't need now for income, but will need to rely on down the road. It's still Green Money because you will rely on it later for income and will need to count on it being there. Need Later Money represents income your assets will need to generate for future use. When planning your retirement, it is vital to decide how much of your assets to structure for income and how much to set aside to accumulate to create Need Later Money.

You must figure out if your income and accumulation needs are met. Your Need Now and Need Later Money are top priorities. Need Now Money, in particular, will dictate what your options for future needs are.

OPTIMIZING RISK AND FINDING THE RIGHT BALANCE

Determining the amount of risk that is right for you depends on your specific situation. It starts by examining your particular financial position.

The Rule of 100 is a useful way to begin to deliberate the right amount of risk for you. But remember, it's just a baseline. Use it as a starting point for figuring out where your money should be. If you're a 50-year-old investor, the Rule of 100 suggests that you have 50 percent Green Money and 50 percent Red Money. Most 50-year-olds are more risk tolerant, however. There are many reasons why someone might be more risk tolerant, not the least of which is feeling young! Experienced investors, people who feel they need to gamble for a higher return, or people who have met their retirement income goals and are looking for additional ways to accumulate wealth are all candidates for investment strategies that incorporate higher levels of risk. In the end, it comes down to your personal tolerance for risk. How much are you willing to lose?

Consulting with a financial professional is often the wisest approach to calculating your risk level. A professional can help determine your risk tolerance by getting to know you, asking you a set of questions and even giving you a survey to determine your comfort level with different types of risk. Here's a typical scenario a financial professional might pose to you:

"*You have $100,000 saved that you would like to invest in the market. There is an investment solution that could turn your $100,000 into $120,000. That same option, however, has the potential of losing you up to $30,000, leaving you with $70,000.*"

Is that a scenario that you are willing to enter into? Or are you more comfortable with this one:

"*You could turn your $100,000 into $110,000, but have the potential of losing $15,000, leaving you with $85,000.*"

Your answer to these and others types of questions will help a financial professional determine what level of risk is right for you. They can then offer you investment strategies and management plans that reflect your financial age.

THE NUMBERS DON'T LIE

When the rubber meets the road, the numbers dictate your options. Your risk tolerance is an important indicator of what kinds of investments you should consider, but if the returns from those investments don't meet your retirement goals, your income needs will likely not be met. For example, if the level of risk you are comfortable with manages your investments at a 4 percent return and you need to realize an 8 percent return, your income needs aren't going to be met when you need to rely on your investments for retirement income. A professional may encourage you to be more aggressive with your investment strategy by taking on more risk in order to give you the potential of earning a greater return. If taking more risk isn't an option that you are comfortable with, then the discussion will turn to how you can earn more money or spend less in order to align your needs with your resources more closely.

How are you going to structure your income flow during retirement? The answer to this question dictates how you determine your risk tolerance. If the numbers say that you need to be more aggressive with your investing, or that you need to modify your lifestyle, it becomes a choice you need to make.

WORKING WITH A FINANCIAL PROFESSIONAL

Take a moment to think about your income goals:
What is your lifestyle today? Would you like to maintain it into retirement? Are you meeting your needs? Are you happy with your lifestyle? What do you really *need* to live on when you retire?

THE COLOR OF MONEY

Some people will have the luxury of maintaining or improving their lifestyle, while others may have to make decisions about what they need versus what they want during their retirement.

Organizing your assets, understanding the color of your money, and creating an income and accumulation plan for retirement can quickly become an overwhelming task. The fact of the matter is that financial professionals build their careers around understanding the different variables affecting retirement financing.

Working with a Registered Investment Advisor means working with a professional who is legally obligated to help you make financial decisions that are in your best interest and fall within your comfort zone. Taking steps toward creating a retirement plan is nothing to take lightly. By leveraging tax strategies, properly organizing your assets, and accumulating helpful financial solutions that help you meet your income and accumulation needs, you are more likely to meet your goals. You might have a million dollars socked away in a savings account, but your neighbor, who has $300,000 in a diverse investment portfolio that is tailored to their needs, may end up enjoying a better retirement lifestyle. Why? They had more than a good work ethic and a penchant for saving. They had a planful approach to retirement-asset allocation.

CHAPTER 2 RECAP //

- Understanding what you own, how each asset works and what risk each asset faces is crucial to your retirement plan.
- There are two types of money: Green and Red. Green Money represents assets that are "safer" and more reliable. Red Money represents assets that are exposed to risk.
- There are two types of Green Money: *Need Now and Need Later*. It is important to structure your investments to provide you with income now and later.
- Working with a Registered Investment Advisor will help you compose a clear and concise inventory of your assets, and learn how much they are worth, what rules apply to them, and how they are structured for risk.
- A Registered Investment Advisor can help you structure your investments so as to reflect your risk tolerance.
- Working with an Investment Advisor means working with a professional who is legally obligated to help you make financial decisions that are in your best interest and fall within your comfort zone.

3
THE BUILDING BLOCKS OF YOUR INCOME PLAN

"If saving money is wrong, I don't want to be right."
— William Shatner

Lois and James came to my office for their first meeting, each holding a stack of shoe boxes in their arms. Inside, I soon learned, were their brokerage account statements. In 2001, when their accounts had plummeted, their broker had told them that they had to hang in there and stay in the market to recover from their losses. They were both age 38 at the time, and they had time to recover, but it was still nerve-racking. The only way they could manage it was to stop opening their statements. They arrived at my office, many years later, ready to plan for retirement. They knew it was time to open the statements and start a new plan, but they weren't looking forward to it.

"I don't think I can do this when I'm retired," Lois told me. "How can we pay our bills or enjoy our retirement if we never know how much money our account will have in it?"

The answer, of course, was simple. They didn't have to do that. Not for even one day of their retirement did Lois and James need to worry about paying their bills. They just needed an income plan.

You ought to enjoy your retirement. You certainly shouldn't be staying up nights and avoiding your mail because your account balance is erratic and frightening. Peace of mind is an indispensible part of a happy retirement, and a key component of that is your income plan.

The first step to creating *an income plan that works for you* is understanding your personal income needs. This is an important and often skipped step. Many people try to rely on a rule of thumb for their income needs, and you'll find a new one in the news every day. Depending on the day and the "expert," the recommendation might be that you need 70 percent of your pre-retirement income to retire, or possibly 130 percent. I recommend that you figure out what *you* need.

Working with your financial professional, you need to go over all your bills, your bank statements, your tax returns, and so forth to figure out what your regular expenses are. Don't stop there, however. After that, it's time to answer some questions.

- What are your plans for the future? Do you plan to travel in the near future? Will you join a golf club or buy a cabin when you retire?
- Will you need to buy a car in the next five years?
- What other big-ticket expenses might arise in the near future? Consider things like your furnace, roof, heating and AC system.
- Do you financially help any of your children?

This isn't an exhaustive list, but the point is to get a thorough understanding of what your future income needs will be. After that, it's time to think about what expenses you'll have in the future. Don't forget to take into account things like healthcare and long-term care options.

A quick note about long-term care: at some point, seven in ten people age 65 or older will need long-term care, defined as personal and medical care required inside or outside your home to maintain healthy living.* Long-term care is necessary for the majority of people at some point, and it is expensive. You have options for how to plan and pay for these costs, and you'd be wise to choose one of them. Long-term care can seriously impact you, or your spouse's, financial situation and standard of living if not planned for properly. Those options might require some of your retirement income to pay premiums, so be sure to discuss this with your financial professional when creating your income plan.

As we determined earlier in Chapter 1, the most important thing you need to do as you create an income plan is to take care to avoid too much exposure to risk. You can start by meeting with an Investment Advisor to organize your assets. Get your Green Money and Red Money in order and balanced to meet your needs. If the market goes down 18 percent this afternoon, you don't want that to come out of what you're relying on for next year's income. Hot on the heels of securing your Green Money, it's time to structure those Green Money assets so they can generate income for you. Ultimately, you have to take care of your monthly income needs to pay the bills.

The Big Kahuna of Green Money is your Social Security benefit.

---

* *http://longtermcare.gov/the-basics/*

CHAPTER 3 RECAP //
- The foundation of a retirement strategy depends on knowing how much money you need and when you need it.
- To determine your true personal income needs, take into account more than just your bills and current monthly expenses. Consider big-ticket items that might need to be purchased as well as healthcare and long-term care expenses.

4
GOVERNMENT SERVICE AND SAVING

"It's not the will to win that matters – everyone has that. It's the will to prepare to win that matters."
– Paul "Bear" Bryant

Retiring as a government employee often requires different steps than for private sector employees. I have made it a point to work with federal employees on a routine basis to help them navigate the government employee retirement system. Through workshops and individual meetings, I take the time to make sure they don't miss out on any of their benefits. I am a Chartered Federal Employee Benefits Consultant (ChFEBC), and have worked with many federal workers to achieve early retirement by helping them figure out how to maximize their benefits at the right time. In most cases, we can show you how to retire on the same income that you had coming in during your working years.

Federal employees have a unique set of options when it comes to retirement planning. If you are a federal employee, or plan on becoming one, this chapter is for you. If not, feel free to move ahead to the next chapter.

There are special sets of rules for federal, state, military, or railroad employees that apply to distribution, survivor benefits, Social Security integration, and taxes.

FEDERAL EMPLOYEES RETIREMENT SYSTEM (FERS)

The majority of federal employees who began work on or after January 1, 1984, are covered by the FERS. The retirement system has three tiers, encompassing benefits provided by
1. Social Security
2. Basic Benefit Plan
3. Thrift Savings Plan

These three tiers work together to support federal employee retirement, like the legs of a stool.

BENEFITS PROVIDED

- **FERS Social Security Benefits.** Previously, federal workers were covered under the Civil Service Retirement Systems (CSRS). Today's FERS employees pay Social Security taxes on their earnings. If you are covered by FERS, you are also entitled to Social Security and Medicare benefits when eligible. It is important to not that your FERS benefits coordinate with your Social Security benefit.
- **Basic Benefit FERS Annuity And Supplement.** The Basic Benefit Plan is at the center of FERS. Retirement, survivor, and disability benefits are paid from this plan to qualified FERS employees, primarily in the form of monthly an-

nuities. Eligibility for benefits hinges on length-of-service requirements and age requirements. Your benefit amount depends on your average pay, your three highest-paying years, and the age you retire. Retirement before Social Security benefit eligibility (at age 62) may make you eligible for a Special Retirement Supplement in addition to your basic annuity. This supplement approximates the Social Security benefit you earned while working as a federal employee and ends when you turn age 62.

Example: Amanda retired at age 60 after 20 years of service as a federal employee. She received her FERS retirement annuity, but was not yet eligible to file for her Social Security benefit. Her basic benefit supplement kicked in, providing her with an additional annuity payment until she turned 62 and became eligible for her Social Security retirement benefits.

ELIGIBILITY REQUIREMENTS

Age and years of service determine eligibility. In some cases, you must have reached Minimum Retirement Age (MRA) to receive retirement benefits. The chart below will help you figure your MRA.

ELIGIBILITY INFORMATION

If You Were Born	Your MRA Is
Before 1948	55
In 1948	55 and 2 months
In 1949	55 and 4 months
In 1950	55 and 6 months
In 1951	55 and 8 months
In 1952	55 and 10 months
In 1953-1964	56
In 1965	56 and 2 months
In 1966	56 and 4 months

In 1967	56 and 6 months
In 1968	56 and 8 months
In 1969	56 and 10 months
In 1970 and after	57

IMMEDIATE RETIREMENT

If you meet one of the following sets of age and service requirements, you might qualify for an immediate retirement benefit. Immediate benefits start within 30 days of your last day of work.

ELIGIBILITY INFORMATION

Age	Years of Service
62	5
60	20
MRA	30
MRA	10

An MRA of at least 10 but less than 30 years of service means a 5 percent reduction of your benefit for each year you are under age 62. If you have 20 years of service and your benefit starts when you reach age 60 or later, however, this does not apply.

RETIRING EARLY

An early retirement benefit is available to federal employees if certain criteria are met. Certain involuntary separations and voluntary separations during major reorganization or reduction in force may allow for early retirement. To be eligible, you must meet the following requirements:

ELIGIBILITY INFORMATION

Age	Years of Service
50	20
Any Age	25

DEFERRING RETIREMENT

If your federal service ends before you have met the age and service requirements for immediate retirement benefits, you may be eligible for deferred retirement benefits. Eligibility requires the completion of at least five years of creditable civilian service. You may receive benefits when you reach one of the following ages:

ELIGIBILITY INFORMATION

Age	Years of Service
62	5
MRA	30
MRA	10

When you retire, if your MRA is at least 10 but less than 30 years of service, you will take a five percent benefit reduction for each year you are under age 62, unless you have 20 years of service and your benefit starts when you reach age 60 or older.

COMPUTATION FOR NON-DISABILITY RETIREMENTS

FERS BASIC ANNUITY FORMULA

Age	Formula
Under age 62 at separation for retirement, or age 62 or older with less than 20 years of service	1 percent of your high 3 average salary for each year of service
Age 62 or older at separation with 20 or more years of service	1.1 percent of your high 3 average salary for each year of service

MILITARY SERVICE

You have the option of purchasing back your military time from the federal government and adding it to your FERS or CSRS annuity. This can be a significant benefit for people who have served our country in the military. The sooner the time is bought back, the cheaper it is to incorporate it into your plan. The following example illustrates the power of this benefit option:

> » Tim is a federal employee age 62 and is looking at retirement this next year. Like we hear so often, Tim was told not to buy his 5 years in the Army back and add them to his federal time. This was so not true. Let's look at the numbers. The cost to Tim buying back his 5 years in the Army today is $6,000. If he buys back this time, his retirement annuity will be $400 more a month for the rest of his life. So if you take the $6000 and divide it by the extra $400 a month Tim will be getting in retirement for the rest of his life, he will recover his $6000 in only 15 months. If he plans on living longer than fifteen months after he retires he will be getting $400 a month more than the cost of buying back that time for every month past the initial fifteen months.

CREDIT FOR MILITARY SERVICE

Military service in the Armed Forces is generally creditable for retirement purposes if the service was active and terminated under honorable conditions. The service also must have been performed prior to your separation from civilian service for retirement.

Service Performed Before 1957
- Creditable without deposit

Service Performed on or after January 1, 1957

GOVERNMENT SERVICE AND SAVING

- A deposit must be paid to credit the service to establish title to an annuity or to compute your annuity

HOW IS FERS FUNDED?

FERS is funded by contributions from both the employee and the federal government. The following table illustrates how FERS is funded:

FERS BENEFIT	EMPLOYEE CONTRIBUTION	FEDERAL GOVERNMENT (EMPLOYER) CONTRIBUTION
SOCIAL SECURITY (INCLUDING MEDICARE)		7.65 PERCENT OF EARNINGS UP TO MAXIMUM WAGE BASE
BASIC BENEFIT PLAN	.80 PERCENT OF EARNINGS	VARIES ACCORDING TO FORMULA
THRIFT SAVINGS PLAN	UP TO 100 PERCENT OF THE BASIC PAY EARNED EACH PAY PERIOD, UP TO THE IRS LIMIT OF %17,500 IN 2013 ($17,000 IN 2012)*	1 PERCENT OF BASIC PAY PLUS $1 OF EVERY DOLLAR EMPLOYEE CONTRIBUTES UP TO 3 PERCENT OF BASIC PAY; 50 CENTS FOR EVERY DOLLAR EMPLOYEE CONTRIBUTES THEREAFTER, UP TO A TOTAL OF 5 PERCENT OF BASIC PAY EACH PAY PERIOD

WHO IS COVERED UNDER FERS?

Almost all federal employees who were hired on or after January 1, 1984, are automatically covered by FERS.

Employees who transfer to FERS from the Civil Service Retirement System may also be covered by FERS. If you elected to transfer to the system from CSRS during a special transfer period in 1987, you may be covered. If you left government service under the CSRS plan, and then returned when FERS was in place, you may also be covered. In this case, you are automatically covered if you left federal government service and returned after more than one year, *and* you have less than five years under CSRS. Special rules may apply, however. For more information about transferring to FERS, you can contact your agency's personnel office or visit this website: www.opm.gov.

EXCLUSION FROM COVERAGE

Some employees are specifically excluded from FERS coverage, including persons not covered by Social Security, employees whose appointments are limited to one year or less, and certain persons with non-federal service that is creditable under the Civil Service Retirement System.

COVER FOR SPECIAL GROUPS

Some special rules apply to the following groups of employees:

GROUP	CONDITIONS	BENEFIT
FIREFIGHTERS, LAW ENFORCEMENT OFFICERS AND AIR TRAFFIC CONTROLLERS	CONTRIBUTE AN EXTRA 0.5 PERCENT OF PAY TO FERS	CAN RECEIVE UNREDUCED BENEFIT AT AGE 50 WITH 20 YEARS OF SERVICE OR AT ANY AGE WITH 25 YEARS OF SERVICE. THE ANNUAL ANNUITY IS 1.7 PERCENT OF HIGH-3 AVERAGE PAY TIMES YEARS OF SERVICE PLUS 1.0 PERCENT OF HIGH-3 AVERAGE PAY TIMES YEARS OF SERVICE EXCEEDING 20

MILITARY RESERVE TECHNICIANS	LOSES MILITARY STATUS REQUIRED TO MAINTAIN POSITION	MAY RETIRE AND RECEIVE AN UNREDUCED ANNUITY IF YOU ARE AT LEAST AGE 50 WITH 25 YEARS OF SERVICE
PART-TIME EMPLOYEES	NONE	IN CALCULATING ANNUITY, AVERAGE HIGH- 3 CONSECUTIVE YEARS OF PAY WILL BE BASED ON FULL-TIME RATE, THEN REDUCED ACCORDING TO PART-TIME SCHEDULE
MEMBERS OF CONGRESS AND CONGRESSIONAL EMPLOYEES	CONTRIBUTE AN EXTRA PERCENT OF PAY TO FERS	MEMBERS OF CONGRESS RECEIVE AN UNREDUCED ANNUITY AT AGE 50 WITH 20 YEARS OF SERVICE OR AT ANY AGE WITH 25 YEARS. CONGRESSIONAL EMPLOYEES ARE SUBJECT TO SAME RULES AS OTHER EMPLOYEES. ANNUITIES FOR BOTH GROUPS WITH AT LEAST 5 YEARS OF CONGRESSIONAL SERVICE WILL BE 1.7 PERCENT OF HIGH-3 AVERAGE PAY TIMES YEARS OF SERVICE UP TO 20 PLUS 1 PERCENT OF HIGH-3 AVERAGE PAY TIMES ANY OTHER SERVICE

FEDERAL THRIFT SAVINGS PLAN

Like a 401(k) plan, the Thrift Savings Plan (TSP) is a savings vehicle for tax-deferred retirement contributions. It is automatically set up for employees under FERS. The government contributes one percent of your basic pay each pay period, and matches a certain amount of contributions you make. Your contributions can be pre-tax or Roth. The TSP annuity is not the basic annuity that you will receive when you retire as either a FERS or CSRS employee, or the retired pay that you receive as a member of the uniformed services.

The TSP was set up to help federal civilian employees and military personnel (as of October 9, 2011) save for retirement.

The Federal Retirement Thrift Investment Board, an independent government agency, administers the plan. Contributions and invested and distributed to employees or service members at retirement or when the employee or service member separates from government service. Benefits are distributed to the employee's or service member's survivors upon their death.

TSP ELIGIBILITY

FERS employees are automatically enrolled in the TSP by their agency. You can file an election to make contributions to your plan at any time. Elections are effective no later than the first full pay period after they are received.

CSRS employees may also contribute to TSPs, but are generally not entitled to Agency Automatic contributions and Agency Matching Contributions. Active-duty and reserve members of the Army, Air Force, Marine Corps, Navy, and Coast Guard, as well as uniformed members of the Public Health Service and the National Oceanic and Atmospheric Administration, can also participate by contributing a portion of their pay to the TSP.

CONTRIBUTING TO A TSP ACCOUNT

Federal employees can generally contribute up to 100 percent of their basic pay to their thrift account each pay period, providing that annual contributions don't exceed the Internal Revenue Code (IRC) elective deferral limit of $17,500. By contributing more, you reduce your gross income, resulting in less income tax on your earnings. Contributions must be made through payroll deductions, and can be made at any time with no waiting period.

Note: If you are a FERS employee hired after July 31, 2010, you are automatically enrolled in the TSP. Three percent of your basic pay will be deducted from your paycheck each pay period as a contribu-

GOVERNMENT SERVICE AND SAVING

tion to your TSP unless you make an election to stop or change your contribution.

Note: Your total elective deferrals to all of your tax-deferred savings plans (including 401(k) and 403(b) plans) cannot exceed the $17,500 annual limit, as of 2013. If you participate in a Section 457(b) plan, however, your contributions to the TSP are not limited by any of your contributions to your section 456(b) plan.

Tip: Military personnel who receive tax-exempt pay can also contribute some or all of that pay to the TSP. Those contributions will remain tax-exempt.

Additionally, non-military TSP participants over the age of 50 can make additional annual payments called "catch-up" contributions. This allows older employees to contribute above regular contribution limits in preparation for retirement. Employees age 50 and older can contribute an additional $5,500 to their TSPs as of 2013. The amount is adjusted annually for inflation.

CONTRIBUTING TO A ROTH

FERS employees may designate all or part of their elective deferrals as Roth contributions. Made on an after-tax basis, these are just like Roth IRA contributions. There is no upfront benefit to contributing in this fashion, but if certain conditions are met, your Roth contributions and earnings can be withdrawn tax-free in the future.

GOVERNMENT CONTRIBUTIONS

The government automatically contributes an amount equal to one percent of your basic pay each pay period to your thrift account whether or not you contribute to the plan or not. These are called Agency Automatic Contributions. Eventually, if you become eligible, your agency will match your contributions up to five percent of the basic pay you contribute each pay period. The first three percent of basic pay is matched dollar-for-dollar, and the remaining two percent is matched at fifty cents on the dollar. **If possible, make sure to take advantage of as much of that "free money" as you can get.**

The TSP is a key component of your FERS retirement. It is in your best interest to contribute as much as you can to it.

Note: CSRS *employees and military personnel generally cannot take advantage of government contributions to their plan.*

TSP INVESTMENT OPTIONS

Any or all of your future contributions to your account can be invested in a TSP "lifecycle" L Fund, or any of the five funds available. The TSP L Funds are designed for individuals who don't want to select or manage their own individual investments. Instead, you have the option of selecting an L Fund that is appropriate for your timeline. L Funds invest in a mix of individual funds available under the TSP and adjusts over time to reflect a lower risk tolerance according to your timeline.

Alternatively, you can invest directly into any or all of the five individual funds offered under the TSP:
- G Fund / Government Securities Investment Fund
- F Fund / Fixed-income Index Fund
- C Fund / Common Stock Index Investment Fund
- S Fund / Small Capitalization Stock Index Invest Fund
- I Fund / International Stock Index Fund

Note: Unlike your TSP, you cannot specify a specific dollar amount to an individual fund. You must select a percentage of your contribution, and not a dollar amount.

TSP FUND DISTRIBUTION

At age 59 ½, participants can take a one-time withdrawal from their TSP. All or a portion of the participant's vested account balance may be withdrawn at that time. A partial account withdrawal makes you ineligible for a partial withdrawal upon separating from service, however.

You may also make in-service withdrawals in the case of financial hardship. Limits and specific requirements apply. A period of six months must pass between withdrawals. Additionally, no contributions can be made to the TSP for a six-month period.

Note: You should carefully consider the consequences of an in-service distribution. Taxable events, penalties, and missed opportunity costs can contribute to the overall depletion of your retirement savings.

When you separate from service, you may take a partial withdrawal of $1,000 or more from your TSP. You can leave the remaining balance in your account until you decide to withdraw it. You may take only one partial distribution from your account, however.

If you elect to take a full withdrawal upon your separation from service, you may receive the full balance of your TSP account in a lump-sum distribution, a series of payments, or through the purchase of an annuity.

You have three types of annuities to choose from:
1. *Single life annuity.* This annuity is paid out to you during your lifetime.
2. *Joint life with spouse annuity.* This type of annuity is paid to you while you and your spouse are alive, then paid to the surviving spouse for the rest of his or her life after one of you passes away.
3. *Joint life with beneficiary annuity.* This annuity is paid to you during your life, and then to a person of your choice (your beneficiary).

Note: You may also choose payment options including cash refund, increasing benefits option, or a 10-year certain feature. If you are a married FERS *participant, you* must *elect a joint life with spouse annuity with a 50 percent survivor benefit, level payments, and no cash refund feature, unless your spouse consents to another annuity option. Additionally, you must have at least $3,500 in your account at the time the TSP uses the money to purchase an annuity. If you don't, you will receive a lump-sum payment.*

PAYMENT AMOUNTS

You monthly annuity payment amount is determined by several factors, including:
- Account balance
- Current interest rate
- Investment fund performance
- Your age (and joint annuitant's age)
- The annuity option you elect

The government provides a calculator on the TSP website (www.tsp.gov) that you can use to project your future account balance, and view tables of approximate annuity payments. There are also private sector options that are beneficial and may be much better for you and your family.

CONSIDERING TAXES

Pre-Tax Contributions

Pre-tax contributions to your TSP account are taken out of your pay before federal (and most state) taxes are calculated. Investment earnings are also tax-deferred. This means that all of the money in your TSP pre-tax account is taxed as ordinary income when you withdraw it.

Roth Contributions

After-tax contributions to your Roth account are not taxed when you withdraw them. They are included in your gross income at the time you contribute to your TSP. Additionally, investment earnings on your Roth contributions grow tax-deferred and may or may not be subject to taxation when they are distributed, depending on whether the distribution is qualified or nonqualified.

Qualified Distributions

If you receive a qualified distribution from your Roth account, the entire amount distributed, both the Roth contributions and investment earnings, is totally free from federal income tax. A qualified distribution is a payment from your Roth account that meets both of the following requirements:

- The payment is made after you turn age 59½, become disabled, or die, and
- The payment is made after the end of the five-year period that starts with the year you make your first Roth contributions to the plan

Nonqualified Distributions

If a payment doesn't satisfy the conditions for a qualified distribution, the portion of the payment that represents the return of your Roth contributions will still be tax-free, but the portion of the payment that represents earnings on those contributions will be subject to income tax and a potential 10 percent premature distribution tax (unless an exception applies). A distribution made before the waiting period has elapsed will always be a nonqualified distribution.

Early Withdrawal

Any taxable amount paid to you from your TSP account before you reach age 59½ may be subject to a 10 percent premature

distribution tax (in addition to the ordinary income tax that you pay on the TSP distribution). However, this additional tax does not apply in certain situations, including the following:
- You separate from service during or after the calendar year in which you reach age 55
- You choose to receive your account balance as an annuity or in monthly payments based on your life expectancy
- You retire on disability
- The payments are made because of death
- Additional exceptions are listed in the Premature Distribution Rule

Saver's tax credit (tax credit for IRAs and retirement plans)
Certain low- and middle-income taxpayers qualify for the saver's tax credit (also known as the tax credit for IRAs and retirement plans). If you participate in the TSP and meet the income requirements, you may be eligible for a tax credit of up to $1,000 on your federal income tax return for each year you participate in the plan.

ADDITIONAL QUESTIONS

Can you borrow money from your TSP?
You may be able to borrow money from your account. However, you'll be expected to repay the loan right away if you leave federal service. The interest you pay will be the G Fund rate in effect at the time your loan application is received. If your loan is considered a general purpose one, you won't be required to document or specify the purpose of your loan. Documentation is required for residential loans only. For more information, contact your personnel office.

Can you roll over an individual retirement account to your TSP?

Whether you are an active or separated federal employee, you can roll over (i.e., transfer) money from a qualified retirement plan or a traditional IRA to your existing TSP account. Money that you are rolling over must be considered an "eligible rollover distribution" under the IRC. If you are separated from service, you can still roll over money to your TSP account unless you have already made a full withdrawal of your account or are receiving monthly payments.

Can you roll over a distribution from your TSP to another plan?

If you (the plan participant) receive an eligible rollover distribution from your TSP, you may roll over all or part of it to an IRA or to another qualified retirement plan, tax-sheltered annuity plan (Section 403(b) plan), or Section 457 plan. (Special rules apply to TSP distributions received by your beneficiaries following your death.) Special rules apply to rollovers from your Roth account.

THE CIVIL SERVICE RETIREMENT SYSTEM (CSRS)

Before FERS, a different retirement system existed for federal employees called the Civil Service Retirement System (CSRS). Federal employees hired by January 1, 1984 were automatically covered by CSRS. The system was created in 1920, and covered most federal employees until FERS was enacted. CSRS employees were given the option to transfer to FERS in 1987.

Employees and the government fund CSRS. Most employees contribute 7 percent of basic pay, and the government agency they work for matches that contribution. The General Treasury provides additional funds for the program.

You must have worked for the federal government for a minimum of five full years to be eligible to receive a CSRS retirement annuity. Additionally, you must have been employed under CSRS for at least one year out of the last two before you retired. An exception exists if you are retiring on disability.

To eligibly retire under the CSRS, you must be:
- Age 55 with 30 years of credible service
- Age 60 with 20 years of credible service
- Age 62 with 5 years of credible service

TYPES OF CSRS RETIREMENT ANNUITIES

When you retire under CSRS, you can elect to receive your annuity in one of three ways:
- Payment of an annuity to you for life
- Payment of an annuity to you for life, with a survivor annuity payable to your spouse for life after you die
- Payment of annuity to you for life, with an insurable interest annuity paid to your beneficiary after you die

The value of your annuity is determined by an equation that includes your length of creditable service and your high-3 average pay. The annuity is computed by adding
- 1.5 percent of your high-3 average pay
- multiplied by service up to 5 years
- plus 1.75 percent of your high-3 average pay
- multiplied by years of service over 5 and up to 10
- plus two percent of your high-3 average pay
- multiplied by years of service over 10

EXAMPLE:
Chelsea's high-3 average pay is $20,000. After 30 years of government service, her annuity is calculated the following way:

    1.5 percent x $20,000 x 5 years   = $ 1,500
    1.75 percent x $20,000 x 5 years   = $ 1,750

2 percent x $20,000 x 20 years = $ 8,000
= $11,250

USING THE CSRS VOLUNTARY CONTRIBUTIONS PROGRAM (VCP)

The CSRS VCP is a creative way to use tax law to achieve a more beneficial financial position for retirement. Essentially, a CSRS VCP allows you to fund a Roth IRA, giving you access to tax-free retirement income. Ask your retirement planning professional how they can assist you with this beneficial strategy.

CHAPTER 4 RECAP //

- Federal employees hired after Jan. 1, 1984, are covered by FERS, a three-tier retirement system that has unique retirements and benefits.
- Federal employees hired before Jan. 1, 1984, and haven't transferred to FERS, are covered by CSRS.
- The Federal Thrift Savings Plan (TSP) is a tax-deferred retirement savings and investment plan, in which employees are eligible to contribute a portion of their annual salary, contributions that may be matched by the government in full or in part.

5

MAKING SENSE OF SOCIAL SECURITY

"The question isn't at what age I want to retire, it's at what income."
– George Foreman

Social Security is a kind of Green Money that many Americans use as the foundation of their retirement income. Unfortunately, filing for Social Security benefits is one of the activities where a large number of retirees make big mistakes. If you're planning to use Social Security benefits as part of your income plan for retirement, you will do yourself a big favor by learning to file the best way possible for you, your spouse and your financial situation.

Filing for Social Security benefits can seem complicated, and you can make a lot of mistakes. The flip side is that there are also a lot of ways you can maximize your lifetime Social Security benefit payments, and you can get expert help to show you how. Let's take a deeper look into Social Security and see what's possible.

> » *Mary had worked full-time nearly her entire adult life and was looking forward to enjoying retirement with her husband, kids and grandkids. When she turned 62, she decided to take advantage of her Social Security benefits as soon as they became available.*
>
> *A couple of years later, she was organizing some of the paperwork in her home office. She came across an old Social Security statement, and remembered the feeling of filing and beginning a new phase in her life.*
>
> *However, as she looked over the statement, she realized in retrospect that she might have been better off waiting to file for benefits. She had saved enough to wait for benefits, and if she had, her monthly benefit could have been quite a bit more.*
>
> *When she was in the process of retiring, there were so many other decisions to make. It seemed very straightforward to file right away. She made a note to call the Social Security Administration to see if it was possible to change her monthly benefit to the larger amount.*

Here are some facts that illustrate how Americans currently use Social Security:
- Nearly 90 percent of Americans age 65 and older receive Social Security benefits.*
- Social Security provides about 39 percent of the income of the elderly.*

---

* *http://www.ssa.gov/pressoffice/basicfact.htm*

- Claiming Social Security benefits at the wrong time can reduce your monthly benefit by up to 65 percent.*
- In 2013, 36 percent of men and 40 percent of women claimed Social Security benefits at age 62.**
- In 2013, more than a third of workers claimed Social Security benefits as soon they became eligible.**
- In 2015, the average monthly Social Security benefit was $1,328. *The maximum benefit for 2015 was $2,663. The $1,335 monthly benefit reduction between the average and the maximum is applied for life.****

There are many aspects of Social Security that are well known and others that aren't. When it comes time for you to cash in on your Social Security benefit, you will have many options and choices. Social Security is a massive government program that manages retirement benefits for millions of people. Experts spend their entire careers understanding and analyzing it. Luckily, you don't have to understand all of the intricacies of Social Security to maximize its advantages. You simply need to know the best way to manage your Social Security benefit. You need to know exactly what to do to get the most from your Social Security benefit and when to do it. Taking the time to create a roadmap for your Social Security strategy will help ensure that you are able to exact your maximum benefit and efficiently coordinate it with the rest of your retirement plan.

There are many aspects of Social Security that you have no control over. You don't control how much you put into it, and

---

* https://www.ssa.gov/planners/retire/retirechart.html

** *Trends in Social Security Claiming*, Alicia H Munnell and Anqi Chen, Center for Retirement Research, May 2015. http://crr.bc.edu/wp-content/uploads/2015/05/IB_15-8.pdf

*** https://www.ssa.gov/news/press/factsheets/colafacts2015.html

you don't control what it's invested in or how the government manages it. However, you do control when and how you file for benefits. The real question about Social Security that you need to answer is, "When should I start taking Social Security?" While this is the all-important question, there are a couple of key pieces of information you need to track down first.

Before we get into a few calculations and strategies that can make all the difference, let's start by covering the basic information about Social Security which should give you an idea of where you stand. Just as the foundation of a house creates the stable platform for the rest of the framework to rest upon, your Social Security benefit is an important part of your overall retirement plan. The purpose of the information that follows is not to give an exhaustive explanation of how Social Security works, but to give you some tools and questions to start understanding how Social Security affects your retirement and how you can prepare for it.

Let's start with eligibility.

Eligibility. Understanding how and when you are eligible for Social Security benefits will help clarify what to expect when the time comes to claim them.

To receive retirement benefits from Social Security, you must earn eligibility. In almost all cases, Americans born after 1929 must earn 40 quarters of credit to be eligible to draw their Social Security retirement benefit. In 2015, a Social Security credit represents $1,220 earned in a calendar quarter. The number changes as it is indexed each year, but not drastically. In 2014, a credit represented $1,200. Four quarters of credit is the maximum number that can be earned each year. In 2015, an American would have had to earn at least $4,880 to accumulate four credits. In order to qualify for retirement benefits, you must have earned a minimum number of credits. Additionally, if you are at least 62 years old and have been married to a recipient of Social Security benefits for at least 12 months, you can choose to receive Spousal Benefits.

Although 40 is the minimum number of credits required to begin drawing benefits, it is important to know that once you claim your Social Security benefit, there is no going back. Although there may be cost of living adjustments made, you are locked into that base benefit amount forever.

Primary Insurance Amount. You can think of your Primary Insurance Amount (PIA) like a ripening fruit. It represents the amount of your Social Security benefit at your Full Retirement Age (FRA). Your benefit becomes fully ripe at your FRA, and will neither reduce nor increase due to early or delayed retirement options. If you opt to take benefits before your FRA, however, your monthly benefit will be less than your PIA. You will essentially be picking an unripe fruit. On the one hand, waiting until after your FRA to access your benefits will increase your benefit beyond your PIA. On the other hand, you don't want the fruit to overripen, because every month you wait is one less check you get from the government.

Full Retirement Age. Your FRA is an important figure for anyone who is planning to rely on Social Security benefits in their retirement. Depending on when you were born, there is a specific age at which you will attain FRA. Your FRA is dictated by your year of birth and is the age at which you can begin receiving your full monthly benefit. Your FRA is important because it is half of the equation used to calculate your Social Security benefit. The other half of the equation is based on when you start taking benefits.

When Social Security was initially set up, the FRA was age 65, and it still is for people born before 1938. But as time has passed, the age for receiving full retirement benefits has increased. If you were born between 1938 and 1960, your full retirement age is somewhere on a sliding scale between 65 and 67. Anyone born in

1960 or later will now have to wait until age 67 for full benefits. Increasing the FRA has helped the government reduce the cost of the Social Security program, which paid out almost $870 billion to beneficiaries in 2015!*

While you can begin collecting benefits as early as age 62, the amount you receive as a monthly benefit will be less than it would be if you wait until you reach or surpass your FRA. It is important to note that if you file for your Social Security benefit before your FRA, **the reduction to your monthly benefit will remain in place for the rest of your life.** You can also delay receiving benefits up to age 70, in which case your benefits will be higher than your PIA for the rest of your life.

- At FRA, 100 percent of PIA is available as a monthly benefit.
- At age 62, your Social Security retirement benefits are available. For each month you take benefits prior to your FRA, however, the monthly amount of your benefit is reduced. ***This reduction stays in place for the rest of your life.***
- At age 70, your monthly benefit reaches its maximum. After you turn age 70, your monthly benefit will no longer increase.

Year of Birth	Full Retirement Age
1943-1954	66
1955	66 and 2 months
1956	66 and 4 months
1957	66 and 6 months
1958	66 and 8 months
1959	66 and 10 months

---

* *https://www.ssa.gov/news/press/basicfact.html*

1960 or later   age 67*

ROLLING UP YOUR SOCIAL SECURITY

Your Social Security income "rolls up" the longer you wait to claim it. Your monthly benefit will continue to increase until you turn 70 years old. Even though Social Security is the foundation of most people's retirement, many Americans feel that they don't have control over how or when they receive their benefits. The truth is that every dollar you increase your Social Security income by means less money you will have to spend from your nest egg to meet your retirement income needs, but many retirees do not take advantage of this fact. For many people, creating their Social Security strategy is the most important decision they can make to positively impact their retirement. ***The difference between the best and worst Social Security decision can be tens of thousands of dollars over a lifetime of benefits.***

Deciding NOW or LATER: Following the above logic, it makes sense to wait as long as you can to begin receiving your Social Security benefit. However, the answer isn't always that simple. Not everyone has the option of waiting. Many people need to rely on Social Security on day one of their retirement. Some might need the income. Others might be in poor health and don't feel they will live long enough to make waiting until their FRA worthwhile for themselves or their families. It is also possible, however, that the majority of folks taking an early benefit at age 62 are simply under-informed about Social Security. Perhaps they make this major decision based on rumors and emotion.

File Immediately if You:
- Find your job is unbearable.
- Are willing to sacrifice retirement income.

---

* *http://www.ssa.gov/OACT/progdata/nra.html*

- Are not healthy and need a reliable source of income.

Consider Delaying Your Benefit if You:
- Want to maximize your retirement income.
- Want to increase retirement benefits for your spouse.
- Are still working and like it.
- Are healthy and willing / able to wait to file.

So if you decide to wait, how long should you wait? Lots of people can put it off for a few years, but not everyone can wait until they are 70 years old. Your individual circumstances may be able to help you determine when you should begin taking Social Security. If you do the math, you will quickly see that between ages 62 and 70, there are 96 months in which you can file for your Social Security benefit. If you take into account those 96 months and the 96 months your spouse could also file for Social Security, and the number of different strategies for structuring your benefit, you can easily end up with more than 20,000 different scenarios. It's safe to say this isn't the kind of math that most people can easily handle. Each month would result in a different benefit amount. The longer you wait, the higher your monthly benefit amount becomes. Each month you wait, however, is one less month that you receive a Social Security check.

The goal is to maximize your lifetime benefits. That may not always mean waiting until you can get the largest monthly payment. Taking the bigger picture into account, you want to find out how to get the most money out of Social Security over the number of years that you draw from it. Don't underestimate the power of optimizing your benefit: the difference between the BEST and WORST Social Security election can easily be worth thousands of dollars in lifetime benefits. *The difference can be very substantial!*

If you know that every month you wait, your Social Security benefit goes up a little bit, and you also know that every month you wait, you receive one less benefit check, how do you determine where the sweet spot is that maximizes your benefits over your lifetime? Financial professionals have access to software that will calculate the best year and month for you to file for benefits based on your default life expectancy. You can further customize that information by estimating your life expectancy based on your health, habits and family history. If you can then create an income plan (we'll get into this later in the chapter) that helps you wait until the target date for you to file for Social Security, you can optimize your retirement income strategy to get the most out of your Social Security benefit. How can you calculate your life expectancy? Well, you don't know exactly how long you'll live, but you have a better idea than the government does. They rely on averages to make their calculations. ***You have much more personal information about your health, lifestyle and family history than they do.*** You can use that knowledge to game the system and beat all the other people who are making uninformed decisions by filing early for Social Security.

While you can and should educate yourself about how Social Security works, the reality is you don't need to know a lot of general information about Social Security in order to make choices about your retirement. What you do need to know is exactly ***what to do to maximize your benefit***. Because knowing what you need to do has huge impacts on your retirement! For most Americans, Social Security is the foundation of income planning for retirement. Social Security benefits represent about 39 percent of the income of the elderly.* For many people, it can represent the largest portion of their retirement income. Not treating your

---

* http://www.socialsecurity.gov/pressoffice/basicfact.htm

Social Security benefit as an asset and investment tool can lead to sub-optimization of your largest source of retirement income. Let's take a look at an example that shows the impact of working with a financial professional to optimize Social Security benefits:

> » *George and Mary Bailey are a typical American couple who have worked their whole lives and saved when they could. George is 60 years old, and Mary is 56 years old. They sat down with a financial professional who logged onto the Social Security website to look up their PIAs. George's PIA is $1,900 and Mary's is $900.*
>
> *If the Baileys cash in at age 62 and begin taking retirement benefits from Social Security, they will receive an estimated $568,600 in lifetime benefits. That may seem like a lot, but if you divide that amount over 20 years, it averages out to around $28,400 per year. The Baileys are accustomed to a more significant annual income than that. To make up the difference, they will have to rely on alternative retirement income options. They will basically have to depend on a bigger nest egg to provide them with the income they need.*
>
> *If they wait until their FRA, they will increase their lifetime benefits to an estimated $609,000. This option allows them to achieve their Primary Insurance Amount, which will provide them a $34,200 annual income.*
>
> *After learning the Baileys' needs and using software to calculate the most optimal time to begin drawing benefits, the Baileys' financial professional determined that the best option for them drastically increases their potential lifetime benefits to $649,000!*
>
> *By using strategies that their financial professional recommended, they increased their potential lifetime benefits by as much as **$80,000**. There's no telling how much you could miss out on from your Social Security if you don't take time to*

create a strategy that calculates your maximum benefit. For the Baileys, the value of maximizing their benefits was the difference between night and day. While this may seem like a special case, it isn't uncommon to find benefit increases of this magnitude. You'll never know unless you take a look at your own options.

Despite the importance of knowing when and how to take your Social Security benefit, many of today's retirees and pre-retirees may know little about the mechanics of Social Security and how they can maximize their benefit.

So, to whom should you turn for advice when making this complex decision? Before you pick up the phone and call Uncle Sam, you should know that the Social Security Administration (SSA) representatives are actually prohibited from giving you election advice! Plus, SSA representatives in general are trained to focus on monthly benefit amounts, not the lifetime income for a family.

MAXIMIZING YOUR LIFETIME BENEFIT

As discussed in Chapter 2, calculating how to maximize **lifetime benefits** is more important than waiting until age 70 for your maximum **monthly benefit amount.** It's about getting the most income during your lifetime. Professional benefit maximization software can target the year and month that it is most beneficial for you to file based on your life expectancy.

The three most common ages that people associate with retirement benefits are 62 (Earliest Eligible Age), 66 (Full Retirement Age), and 70 (age at which monthly maximum benefit is reached). In almost all circumstances, however, none of those three most common ages will give you the maximum lifetime benefit.

Remember, every month you wait to file, the amount of your benefit check goes up, but you also get one less check. You don't know how exactly how long you're going to live, but you have a better idea of your life expectancy than the actuaries at the Social Security Administration who can only work with averages. They can't make calculations based on your specific situation. A professional can run the numbers for you and get the target date that maximizes your potential lifetime benefits. You can't get this information from the SSA, but you *can* get it from a financial professional.

Types of Social Security Benefits:
- *Retired Worker Benefit.* This is the benefit with which most people are familiar. The Retired Worker Benefit is what most people are talking about when they refer to Social Security. It is your benefit based on your earnings and the amount that you have paid into the system over the span of your career.
- *Spousal Benefit.* This is available to the spouse of someone who is eligible for Retired Worker Benefits.
- *Survivorship Benefit.* When one spouse passes away, the survivor is able to receive the larger of the two benefit amounts.
- *Restricted Application.* A higher-earning spouse may be able to start collecting a spousal benefit on the lower-earning spouse's benefit while allowing his or her benefit to continue to grow. Due to the Bipartisan Budget Act of 2015, this option is only available to individuals who turned age 62 before January 1, 2016.

In November of 2015, the Bipartisan Budget Act of 2015 was passed, which will have a dramatic impact on the way many Americans plan for Social Security. As the largest change to Social Security since 2000, the Bipartisan Budget Act of 2015 eliminated an estimated $9.5 billion* of benefits to retirees and may limit some of the flexibility you previously had to structure your benefits.

In 2000, Congress passed the Senior Citizens Freedom to Work Act. The bill allowed retirees to suspend receiving benefits so they wouldn't be subject to additional taxation if they chose to return to work after they filed for Social Security. However, by doing so, the bill also unintentionally created several loopholes in claiming strategies: most notably, the Restricted Application for spousal benefits and "file and suspend" filing strategy. For most Americans, the Bipartisan Budget Act of 2015 closed these loopholes by eliminating "file and suspend" and the Restricted Application.

The new rules mandate that:
- If a primary worker is not currently receiving benefits, then their dependents (child, spouse) can no longer collect benefits based on the primary worker's earning record.
- If you file for benefits, then you are filing for *all* benefits to which you are entitled—not just the benefit type you choose.

It's important to remember that in spite of these immense changes, one thing stayed the same—filing for Social Security is one of the most important financial decisions you will make in your lifetime, and a financial professional can help ensure you make the right one.

---

* *http://www.nasdaq.com/article/congress-planning-to-close-social-security-loopholes-cm536252*

THE DIVORCE FACTOR

How does a divorced spouse qualify for benefits? If you have gone through a divorce, it might affect the retirement benefit to which you are entitled.

In general, a person can receive benefits as a divorced spouse on a former spouse's Social Security record so long as the following conditions are met:
- the marriage lasted at least 10 years; and
- the person filing for divorce benefits is at least age 62, unmarried, and not entitled to a higher Social Security benefit on his or her own record.*

With all of the different options, strategies and benefits to choose from, you can see why filing for Social Security is more complicated than just mailing in the paperwork. Gathering the data and making yourself aware of all your different options isn't enough to know exactly what to do, however. On the one hand, you can knock yourself out trying to figure out which options are best for you and wondering if you made the best decision. On the other hand, you can work with a financial professional who uses customized software that takes all the variables of your specific situation into account and calculates your best option. You have tens of thousands of different options for filing for your Social Security benefit. If your spouse is a different age than you are, it nearly doubles the amount of options you have. This is far more complicated arithmetic than most people can do on their own. If you want a truly accurate understanding of when and how to file, you need someone who will ask you the right questions about your situation, someone who has access to specialized software that can crunch the numbers. The reality is that you need to work with a professional that can provide you with the sophisticated

---

* http://www.ssa.gov/retire2/yourdivspouse.htm

analysis of your situation that will help you make a truly informed decision.

Important Questions about Your Social Security Benefit:
- *How can I maximize my lifetime benefit?* By knowing when and how to file for Social Security. This usually means waiting until you have at least reached your Full Retirement Age. A professional has the experience and the tools to help determine when and how you can maximize your lifetime benefits.
- *Who will provide reliable advice for making these decisions?* Only a professional has the tools and experience to provide you reliable advice.
- *Will the Social Security Administration provide me with the advice?* The Social Security Administration cannot provide you with advice or strategies for claiming your benefit. They can give you information about your monthly benefit, but that's it. They also don't have the tools to tell you what your specific best option is. They can accurately answer how the system works, but they can't advise you on what decision to make as to how and when to file for benefits.

The Maximization Report that your financial professional will generate represents an invaluable resource for understanding how and when to file for your Social Security benefit. When you get your customized Social Security Maximization Report, you will not only know all the options available to you—but you will understand the financial implications of each choice. In addition to the analysis, you will also get a report that shows *exactly* at what age—including which month and year—you should trigger benefits and how you should apply. It also includes a variety of other time-specific recommendations, such as when to apply for

Medicare or take Required Minimum Distributions from your qualified plans. A report means there is no need to wonder, or to try to figure out when to take action—the Social Security Maximization Report lays it all out for you in plain English.

PENSIONS

The age of the defined benefit plan, or pension, is fading. We all know this. But enough people still receive pensions for it to warrant some discussion. Add to that the fact that more and more employees who receive pensions have also been receiving pension buyout, or lump sum, offers from their employers, and that creates a complicated question for retirees. What is the best option for you?

Your options. When it's time to elect your pension options, the situation is often similar to electing Social Security benefits: once you make them, there is usually only a small grace period, if any, in which to make changes. It's a good idea to seek expert advice.

Your spouse. In most cases, the person receiving the pension will have the opportunity to elect to receive a smaller monthly payment in exchange for spousal continuation when the pension owner passes away. Give this some serious thought, and if you feel strongly that you require the higher amount, be sure you put an alternative plan in place to replace potentially lost income for your spouse.

Your advisor. If you're offered a buyout option, it's always best to seek expert help to run the numbers. For one thing, some buyout offers are sounder than others. For another, the best decision is the one that works in concert with your overall financial goals and plan. Ideally, the person who is helping you create and execute that plan will assist with your pension options.

CHAPTER 5 RECAP //
- To get the most out of your Social Security benefit, you need to file at the right time.
- An Investment Advisor can help you determine when you should file for Social Security to get your Maximum Lifetime Benefit.
- Filing for Social Security benefits is a complex decision with many different options that can affect your overall lifetime income.
- Many retirees don't realize that they have Social Security benefit filing options beyond just filing at age 62, 66, or 70.
- Choosing the right filing options for you and filing at the right time can make a significant difference in your overall lifetime benefit.
- Employees of the Social Security Administration can only provide you with your benefit amount; they are prohibited from offering advice on filing options.
- An Investment Advisor can help you determine how to file to receive your maximum lifetime Social Security benefit, as well as advise you on your pension options, if necessary.

6
WHEN SOCIAL SECURITY ISN'T ENOUGH

"Money is a good servant, but a bad master."
— H.G. Bohn

Angelica and Miles had met when they were 18 years old. It was the first day of college, and Miles was frustrated with the long line he had to stand in to register for classes. After a half hour, he'd had enough. He turned around and started to walk out of the line, but a hand reached out and grabbed his arm. "Where do you think you're going?" demanded the short girl with sparkling brown eyes behind him.

"Um, I was... leaving... I guess. I have better things to do than to wait in this stupid line."

Angelica laughed. "No, you don't."

> Three years later, they were married, and they'd been together for decades by the time they appeared in my office, worried about their Social Security benefits.
>
> "I'm not in great health," Angelica explained, "and I think we should take my Social Security benefit as soon as possible. I just want to be sure Miles is taken care of if anything happens to me, and I worry about him depending on our stock portfolio. It's been up and down so many times over the years."
>
> Of course, Miles was just as concerned about how Angelica would manage without him, and they were both looking to Social Security benefits to help them out with that worry."
>
> I had even better news for them. "You can both stop worrying right now. Social Security is only one component of your lifetime income plan. If dependable income is what you're looking for, we have lots of options for filling your income gap. I'll work with you to find the one that fits your exact needs."

It's true that Social Security benefits are a reliable, critical source of retirement income for many people: 52 percent of married couples and 74 percent of unmarried persons receive at least half of their retirement income from Social Security.* That's only half of their income, however. The difference between your income needs and your Social Security benefit is what we call your "Income Gap." As part of your retirement plan, we look at ways to leverage your other retirement assets (your IRA, Roth IRA, 401(k), stock holdings, real estate, etc.) to generate income to fill that gap. As we discussed in Chapter 1, there was a time when the general retirement wisdom was to leave your money in the stock market and withdraw a certain percentage every year or month. But with the stock market soaring and plummeting regularly,

---

* http://www.ssa.gov/news/press/basicfact.html

many retirees like Miles and Angelica prefer less stressful, more dependable ways to cover their income needs.

If you have a known income gap that you need to fill, you want to know how to fill that income gap with the fewest dollars possible. You basically want to buy that income gap for the least amount of money possible. You don't want it to cost you too much, because you want to get the most out of your other assets, including planning for your future and planning for your legacy. You do that by maximizing your Social Security benefit, leveraging your additional income and looking at other investment tools that can help generate income for you. A professional, of course, should analyze your specific needs.

TAKING A HYBRID APPROACH TO YOUR INCOME NEEDS

You looked at Social Security strategies earlier, discovering you have some control over how and when you file. Those decisions can change the outcome of your benefit in your favor. Once you start drawing that income, it is safer and will provide you with a reliable source of income for the rest of your life. While there are many factors of Social Security that you can control, there are many that you cannot.

For example, you do not have the choice of putting more money into Social Security in order to get more out of it. If you could have the option to contribute more money toward Social Security in order to secure a guaranteed income, it would be a great way to create a Green Money asset that would enhance your retirement. Since that option isn't available, you may seek an investment tool that is similar to Social Security that provides you with a reliable income. It also has the potential to increase the value of your principal investment! This kind of win-win situation exists, and it's called a Fixed Index Annuity.

Before we get to that, let's take a step back and look at annuities in general. There are a lot of different kinds of annuities, and each of them has pros and cons. What's more, there are a lot of misconceptions about annuities. Take Wallace, for example:

> *Wallace was 72 years old when another client referred him to me. He had a problem: he had an annuity and was receiving regular checks from that annuity, but he kept receiving confusing statements that showed his annuity losing money. The checks kept coming, so he didn't worry for a while. But as his principal balance dipped lower and lower, anxiety crept in. Finally, he talked to his neighbor, who happened to be a client of mine and told him to come see me.*
>
> *"I bought this because the agent told me I would receive an income for the rest of my life," Wallace told me. "He also said it was guaranteed to earn 6 percent every year, but I can see that that's not happening. I just don't understand why."*
>
> *Wallace showed me all of his statements, and the problem became clear right away. I decided to call the insurance company right then, with Wallace in the room, so he could hear the information straight from the source.*
>
> *During that call, the representative told Wallace what he really needed to know. What he owned was a variable annuity with an income rider. As such, it was exposed to market risk, and his principal had been taking major losses. What's more, he was paying such high fees that they almost always outweighed any growth the account achieved.*
>
> *By the time Wallace came to see me, his principal was so low that it made more sense to keep the income guaranteed by his rider than to cash out. Fortunately, the annuity was just one part of the assets Wallace had accumulated, and the income from his rider was ample to continue covering his needs.*

Wallace isn't alone. I meet people every week who think they own one type of solution, but actually own something quite different. Either their principals aren't quite as "safe" as they thought or they are paying fees much higher than they realized. What it comes down to, in most cases, is understanding the type of annuity you are purchasing and how it works to solve your particular problem.

TYPES OF ANNUITIES

An annuity is a contract between you and an insurance company. You agree to give the insurance company a certain amount of money, and the insurance company invests that money. But make no mistake: just because an annuity is purchased from an insurance company, it doesn't mean that your money is always "insured." Sometimes your principal, the amount you paid to buy the annuity, is guaranteed, and sometimes it's not. There are a number of different specific types of annuities, but in general, they can be divided into categories by two things: when you will receive payments, and how the annuity will earn interest.

Immediate annuities begin paying you right away. Deferred annuities accumulate value for a set period of time (the amount of time depending on your specific contract) before you begin receiving payments. Additionally, different types of annuities earn income in different ways:

- Fixed annuities work similarly to bank CDs. Instead of buying them from banks, you buy them from insurance companies. A fixed annuity earns interest based on a fixed rate over an agreed-upon contract period.
- Indexed annuities are tied to a particular equities index, such as the Dow Jones Industrial Average (DJIA) or the Standard & Poor's (S&P) 500, and earn interest based on how those indices perform. These indexed annuities fall into two basic categories:

» *Variable annuities.* These are commonly misunderstood because they are called "annuities" and yet they behave more like securities. Variable annuities can offer growth potential because they are tied to an index, but they also present risk. Their principals are not guaranteed, and they tend of have higher fees than many other annuities.

» *Fixed Index Annuities (FIA).* This type of annuity is a hybrid of the fixed annuity and the variable annuity. While FIAs are tied to an index, they have a fixed top and bottom. The "top" is a cap that means you can only earn a certain amount of an index's growth, and the "bottom" is zero: their principal cannot go down. One of the newest kinds of annuities, FIAs, offer both growth potential and safety.

Within all annuities, there are many variables in your contract with the insurance company that can significantly affect how it performs. Consider the following examples:

- **Cap.** The "cap" is the maximum amount of interest your annuity can earn over a set period of time. For example, if your cap is 6 percent each month, and your index earns 12 percent, your annuity will still only earn 6 percent.
- **Spread.** Some annuities also have a spread, which is a set percentage that is always subtracted from any gain your annuity's index receives. Example: if your fixed index annuity has a 2 percent spread, and the index makes an 8 percent gain, your annuity earns 6 percent.
- **Annual reset.** Annual reset is a unique feature of some annuities. It means that all of the interest the annuity earned during the year gets added to the principal in the following year and locked in. Not only does that mean you earn compound interest (a greater principal gener-

ates more interest), but also, it means that your interest becomes part of that guaranteed principal that cannot be lost. If your annuity earns 4 percent interest this year, that interest gets locked in and cannot be lost, even if your index takes a hit.

Now that we've covered the basics of annuities, let's turn back to that Fixed Index Annuity, that win-win solution that can offer you guaranteed income and the potential to increase the value of your principal investment.

HOW FIXED INDEX ANNUITIES FIT INTO AN OVERALL INCOME PLAN

Annuities are popular and reliable investment tools that allow you to secure income during retirement. In its simplest form, an annuity is a way to invest your money that allows you to structure it for income. Annuities come in a variety of modes. Finding the right one for you will take a conversation with your financial professional. Be sure you fully understand the features, benefits and costs of any annuity you are considering before investing money.

Here is how they can work:

Let's say you have saved $100,000 and need it to generate income to meet your needs above and beyond your Social Security and pension checks. You give the $100,000 to an insurance company, who in turn invests it to generate growth.

They usually select investments that have modest returns over long-term horizons. In other words, they generally put it somewhere that could be potentially more stable and predictable. Most commonly, they will invest it in a combination of bonds and treasuries that are safer and dependable ways to grow money. They use the money from the insurance solutions they sell to invest, use a portion of the returns to generate profits for themselves, and return a portion to clients in the form of payouts, claims, and structured income options.

INCOME RIDER

When you use that $100,000 to buy a contract with an insurance company in the form of a fixed index annuity, you are pegging your money on an index. It could be the S&P 500, the Dow Jones Industrial Average or any number of indexes. To generate income from this annuity, you select something called an income rider. An income rider is a subset of an indexed annuity. Essentially, it is the amount of money from which the insurance company will pay you an income while you have your money in their annuity. Your income rider is a larger number than what your investment is actually worth, and if you select the income rider, it will increase in value over time, providing you with more income. As the insurance company holds your money and invests it, they generate a return on it that they use to pay you a regular monthly income based on a higher number. The insurance company has to outperform the amount that they pay you in order to make a profit.

Remember, insurance companies make long-term investments that provide them with predictable flows of money. They like to stabilize the amount of money that goes in and out of their doors instead of paying and receiving large unpredictable chunks at once. When you opt for an income rider, an insurance company can reliably predict how much money they will pay out to you over a set period of time. It's predictable, and they like that. They can base their business on those predictable numbers.

In order to encourage investors to leave their money in their fixed annuity contracts, insurance companies create surrender periods that protect their investments. If you remove your money from the fixed annuity contract during the surrender period, you will pay a penalty and will not be able to receive your entire investment amount back. A typical surrender period is 10 years. If after three years you decide that you want your $100,000 back, the insurance company has that money tied up in bonds and other investments with the understanding that they will have it for another seven years. Because they will take a hit on removing the money from their investments prematurely, you will have to pay a surrender charge that makes up for their loss.

The higher returns that you are guaranteed from a fixed annuity are dependent on the timeframe you selected. The longer an insurance company can hold your money, the easier it is for them to guarantee a predictable return on it.

If you leave your money in the fixed annuity contract, you get a reliable monthly income no matter what happens in the market. Once the surrender period has expired, you can remove your money whenever you want. Your money becomes liquid again

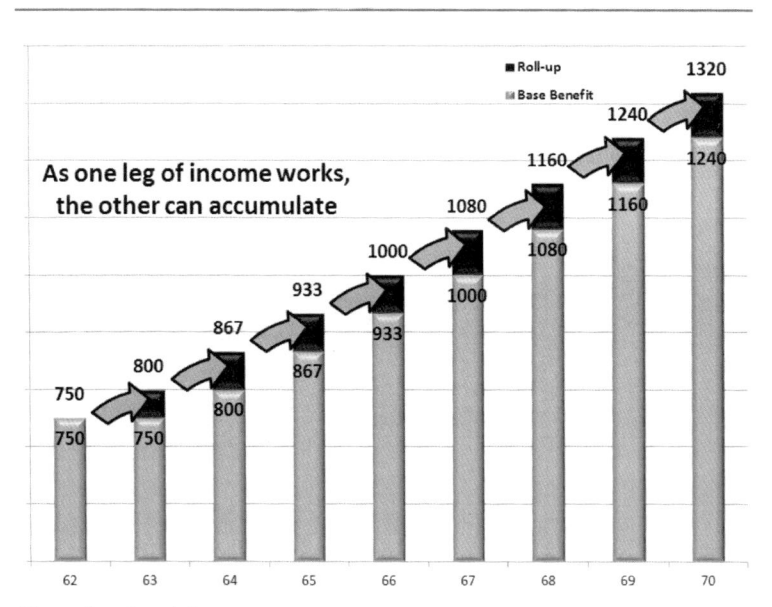

This is a hypothetical illustration

because the insurance company has used it in an investment that fit the timeline of your surrender period. For many people, this is an attractive trade off that can provide a creative solution for filling their income gap.

When is a fixed annuity with an income rider right for you? Before you make that decision, it is imperative that you understand the pros and cons. Each financial product has a set of characteristics that can contribute positively or negatively to your portfolio depending on your needs. For example, let's look at a Fixed Index Annuity:

PROS
- Protection of principal
- Opportunity to participate in the growth potential of an index without the risk of the market's downside
- Riders allow you to leverage your assets to solve other issues, such as long-term healthcare coverage or spousal income continuation
- Control over how your legacy is received

CONS
- Access to money is limited to 10 percent of principal per year
- Contract terms are long: 7, 10, or 12 years for example
- Caps limit how much you are able to participate in market upsides

Take a look at the cons. If a Fixed Index Annuity is right for you, they won't seem so much like cons. If you need access to your full principal in the next 10-15 years, for example, a Fixed Index Annuity is likely not the right solution for you. Also, a cap might seem like a con if you feel that you need to earn higher returns. Remember, however, the lower returns created by the cap are balanced by the fact that during time of negative market returns, your annuity would lose nothing.

Anytime you are choosing a financial solution, annuity or otherwise, it's best to seek the advice of your financial professional. The professional who understands your entire financial picture and plan is best equipped to help you make a decision that fits your overall goals. You are looking for the piece that fits your individual retirement puzzle. There's no one-size solution for everyone.

Some people need income today; others need it in five or 10 years. Others may have their income needs met but are planning to move closer to their children and will need to buy a house in 10 years. Or, if you want income in 15 years, you might want to choose a different investment solution for 10 years, and then switch to a fixed annuity with an income rider during the last five years of your timeline. Everyone's situation is different and everyone's needs are different. People who are interested in annuities, however, usually need to make decisions that affect their income needs, whether it is filling their income gap, or providing for income down the road.

What happens if you place on a shorter timeframe those assets from which you need to draw an income? Something called single premium immediate annuities may be for you:

SINGLE PREMIUM IMMEDIATE ANNUITIES (SPIA)

A single premium immediate fixed annuity is simply a contract between you and an insurance company. SPIAs are structured so that you pay a lump sum of money (a single premium) to an insurance company, and they give you a guaranteed income over an agreed upon time period. That time period could be five years, or it could be for the remainder of your lifetime. Guarantees from insurance companies are based on the claims-paying ability of the issuing insurance company.

SPIAs provide investors with a stream of reliable income when they can't afford to take the risk of losing money in a fluctuating market. While there is general faith that the market always trends up, at least in the long-term, if you are focusing on income over a shorter period of time, you may not be able to take a big hit in the market. Beyond normal market volatility, interest rates also come with an inherent level of uncertainty, making it hard to create a dependable income on your own. SPIAs reduce risk for you by giving you regular monthly, quarterly or yearly payments that can begin the moment you buy the contract. Your financial professional can walk you through a series of different payment options to help you select the one that most closely fits your needs.

Additional Fixed Annuity Information:
- Some contracts will allow you to draw income from the high water mark that the market reaches each year. The income rider will then begin calculating its value from the high water mark.
- Variable annuities, however, can lose money with market fluctuations. As their name suggests, they vary with the market. These annuities do not take advantage of annual reset when the market goes down. The income rider will stay the same, but the value of your actual contract may fall. If you surrender the variable annuity, the insurance company will pay you the market value of the asset, regardless of whether it matches, exceeds or falls short of the value at which you bought the contract. If its value has dropped significantly, you may be better off taking the income rider without surrendering your contract.
- Every year you allow the money to grow with the market, and it will "roll up" by a specific amount, paying out a specific percent to you as income each year.

- Annuities can work very well to create income, and a financial professional can help you find the one that best matches your income need, and can also structure it to work perfectly for you.

Managing Risk Within Your Annuity:
Just like any investment strategy, the amount of risk needs to fit the comfort level of the investor. Annuities are no exception. Without going into too much detail, here are some additional ways to manage risk with annuity options:
- If you want to structure an annuity investment for growth over a long period of time, you can select a variable annuity. The value of your principal investment follows the market and can lose or gain value with the market. This type of annuity can also have an income rider, but it is really more useful as an accumulation tool that bets on an improving market. A 40-year-old couple, for example, will probably want to structure more for growth and take on more risk than someone in their 70s. The 40-year-old couple may select a variable annuity with an income rider that kicks in when they plan to retire. If it rises with the market or outperforms it, the value of their investment has grown. If the market loses ground over the duration of the contract or their annuity underperforms, they can still rely on the income rider.
- If you are 68 years old and you have more immediate income needs that you need to come up with above and beyond your Social Security, you need a low risk, reliable source of income. If you choose an annuity option, you are looking for something that will pay out an income right away over a relatively short timeframe. You probably want to opt for a SPIA that pays you immediately and spans a five-year period, as well as an additional annuity

that begins paying you in five years, and another longer-term annuity that begins paying you in 10 years. Bear in mind that each annuity contract has its own costs and fees. Review these with your financial professional before you determine the best solutions and strategies for your situation.

Some questions to ask if you're considering an annuity:
- **What are the terms of my contract?** Your contract terms determine exactly how your annuity will operate, when you will have access to your principal and how much you can withdraw, how much this annuity will cost each year, and much more. You need to be aware of every detail of this contract before you sign on the dotted line. A second opinion is always helpful, and your investment advisor is a good person to ask.
- **Can I trust this insurance company?** Occasionally, a client only wants to work with a certain company, perhaps because they have read something they liked about that company, or because they already work with that company on other insurance policies. Be careful about how you are evaluating the company you are considering working with. Even if you really like one company, take a look at all of your options. There might be a company out there that offers the perfect contract for your needs, and it would be a shame to miss out on that because you didn't review your options.
- **How is the company rated?** There are credit ratings for insurance companies that help you determine whether they will be able to make good on their end of your contract in the long run. These are important, but it's also important to consider why a company has recently been downgraded before writing them off as an option.

For example, a company might acquire a competitor that hasn't been performing as well, and therefore the parent company will be downgraded for a while because of the purchase. That doesn't necessarily mean that the insurance company won't be able to uphold its end of your contract. It might simply mean that the company is motivated to be more flexible, for a short period of time, about some contract details.

Working with an investment advisor who has great strategic partnerships can help you choose an insurance company you can trust. I work with Gradient Financial Group, LLC to research all of my clients' options because I believe that a second opinion is good for everyone, even your advisor.

The following example shows just how helpful an indexed annuity option can be for a retiree:

> » *Bob and Mary are 62 years old and have decided to run the numbers to see what their retirement is going to look like. They know they currently need $6,000 per month to pay their bills and maintain their current lifestyle. They have also done their Social Security homework and have determined that, between the two of them, they will receive $4,200 per month in benefits. They also receive $350 per month in rent from a tenant who lives in a small carriage house in their backyard. Between their Social Security and the monthly rent income, they will be short $1,450 per month.*
>
> *They do have an additional asset, however. They have been contributing for years to an IRA that has reached a value of $350,000. They realize that they have to figure out how to turn the $350,000 in their IRA into $1,450 per month for the rest of their life. At first glance, it may seem like they will have plenty of money. With some quick calculations, they find*

they have 240 months, or nearly 20 years, of monthly income before they exhaust the account. When you consider income tax, the potential for higher taxes in the future, and market fluctuations (because many IRAs are invested in the market), the amount in the IRA seems to have a little less clout. Every dollar Bob and Mary take out of the IRA is subject to income tax, and if they leave the remainder in the IRA, they run the risk of losing money in a volatile market. Once they retire and stop getting a paycheck every two weeks, they also stop contributing to their IRA. And when they aren't supplementing its growth with their own money, they are entirely dependent on market growth. That's a scary prospect. They could also withdraw the money from the IRA and put it in a savings account or CD, but removing all the money at once will put them in a tax bracket that will claim a huge portion of the value of the IRA. A seemingly straightforward asset has now become a complicated equation. Bob and Mary didn't know what to do, so they met with their financial professional.

Their financial professional suggested that they use the money to purchase a fixed indexed annuity with an income rider. They selected an annuity that was designed for their specific situation. They took the lump sum from their IRA, placed it in an indexed annuity taking advantage of annual reset so they never lost the value of their investment. In return, they were guaranteed the $1,450 of income per month that they needed to meet their retirement goals. Their professional was able to find a fixed indexed annuity for them that allowed them their $1,450 monthly payment with a lump sum of $249,455, leaving them more than $100,000 to reinvest somewhere else. Keep in mind that annuities are tax deferred, meaning you will pay tax on the income you receive from an annuity in the year you receive it.

» *Tanya is 60 years old and is wondering how she can use her assets to provide her with a retirement income. She has a $5,000 per month income need. If she starts withdrawing her Social Security benefit in six years at age 66, it will provide her with $2,200 per month. She also has a pension that kicks in at age 70 that will give her another $1,320 per month.*

That leaves an income gap of $2,800 from ages 66 to 69, and then an income gap of $1,480 at age 70 and beyond. If Tanya uses only Green Money to solve her income need, she will need to deposit $918,360 at two percent interest to meet her monthly goal for her lifetime. If she opts to use Red Money and withdraws the amount she needs each month from the market, let's say the S&P 500, she will run out of cash in 10 years if she invested between the years of 2000 and 2012. Suffering a market downturn like that during the period for which she is relying on it for retirement income will change her life, and not for the better.

Working with a financial professional to find a better way, Tanya found that she could take a hybrid approach to fill her income gap. Her professional recommended two different income vehicles: one that allowed her to deposit just $190,161 with a 2 percent return, and one that was a $146,000 fixed annuity. These tools filled her income gap with $336,161, requiring her to spend $582,000 less money to accomplish her goal! Working with a professional to find the right tools for her retirement needs saved Tanya over half a million dollars.

CREATING AN INCOME PLAN

Creating an income plan before you retire allows you to satisfy your need for lifetime income and ensures that your lifestyle can last as long as you do. You also want to create a plan that operates in the most efficient way possible. Doing so will give more security to your Need Later Money and will potentially allow you to build your legacy down the road.

Here is a basic roadmap of what we have covered so far:
- Review your income needs and look specifically at the shortfall you may have during each year of your retirement based on your Social Security income, and income from any other assets you have.
- Ask yourself where you are in your distribution phase. Is retirement one year away? 10 years away? Last year?
- Determine how much money you need and how you need to structure your existing assets to provide for that need.
- If you have an asset from which you need to generate income, consider options offered by purchasing an income rider on a fixed annuity.

» Jeanne wants to retire at age 68. However, after her Social Security benefit, she will need nearly $375,000 in assets to generate a modest $40,000 of income per year.

Amazingly, most people don't look ahead to think that at 68 years old, they will need $375,000 to have a basic lifestyle that pays out around $40,000 with Social Security benefits.

CHAPTER 6 RECAP //

- After Social Security and your additional income are accounted for, the amount that's left to meet your needs is called the *Income Gap*.
- Many retirees prefer to finds ways to leverage their other assets to create sources of reliable retirement income.
- It has been ages since many stocks returned meaningful dividends, so it isn't advisable to rely on them for essential income. However, without stocks, your retirement plan will likely lose ground to inflation.
- It might be very attractive to have another asset, such as an annuity, that is designed to give you lifetime income. That income can go up in value as you wait to trigger a monthly check.
- If you think maximizing your Social Security isn't enough and you need the rest of your assets to be optimized to fill the income gap, an annuity may be a good option for you.
- Although an annuity is an income-producing asset that does not subject your income to market risk, it still has the opportunity to grow.
- You should always examine the pros and cons of any financial solution before you invest. There is no financial solution that is right for everyone.
- It is also a good idea to discuss your options with the financial professional who is helping you create your overall retirement plan and therefore understands your goals and situation.

7
WHAT ARE YOUR OPTIONS FOR GROWTH?

"Investing should be more like watching paint dry or watching grass grow. If you want excitement, take $800 and go to Las Vegas."
– Paul Samuelson

Understanding your Social Security benefit, filling the income gap and making an overall plan that meets your retirement income needs is no small task. Once you have worked with a financial professional to structure your income needs, it's time to take a look at the future. With your immediate income needs met, you have the opportunity to take your additional assets and leverage them for profit to supplement your income in the future, to prepare for anticipated health care costs or to contribute to your legacy. Stable income also means that you should have the staying power to stick with your investment portfolio through the ups and downs in the market.

MATH OF REBOUNDS

A fickle market can raise the eyebrows of even the most veteran investor. Taking a hit in the market hurts no matter how stable your income. Part of the pain comes from knowing that when you take a step back in the market, it requires an even larger step forward to return to where you were. As the market goes up and down, those larger gains you need to realize to get back to zero start to look even more daunting. I believe that the worst time to lose money in your retirement nest egg is during the last 5 of your working years and the first 5 of your retirement years. This is because your time to make the losses back up is diminished.

HOW REAL PEOPLE MAKE INVESTMENT DECISIONS

It can be challenging to watch the stock market's erratic changes every month, week or even every day. When you have your money riding on it, the ride can feel pretty bumpy. When you are managing your money by yourself, emotions inevitably enter into the mix. The Dow Jones Industrial Average and the S&P 500 represent more to you than market fluctuations. They represent a portion of your retirement. It's hard not to be emotional about it.

Everyone knows you should buy low and sell high. But this is what is more likely to happen:

The market takes a downturn, similar to the 2008 crash, and investors see as much as a 30 percent loss in their stock holdings. It's hard to watch, and it's harder to bear the pain of losing that much money. The math of rebounds means that they will need to rely on even larger gains just to get back to where things were before the downturn. They sell. But eventually, and inevitably, the market begins to rise again. Maybe slowly, maybe with some moderate growth, but by the time the average investor notices an upward trend and wants to buy in again, they have already missed a great deal of the gains.

CHAPTER 7 RECAP //

- When you have a stable plan in place to provide you income, you can consider positioning your remaining assets to provide growth for your future income.
- Remember the Math of Rebounds: every market loss requires an even larger gain just to get back to zero.
- Most people know you should buy low and sell high, but when your savings are on the line, it can be hard to react without emotion. That's just one of several reasons you should consider using a professional money manager as part of your overall retirement plan.

8
AVOIDING EMOTIONAL INVESTING

*"The most important thing to do if you find
yourself in a hole is to stop digging."*
– Warren Buffett

Megan's situation illustrates how market volatility can have major repercussions for an individual investor.

After her children started school, Megan went back to work and was delighted to get an engineering job at a major automotive company in Detroit. During her many years there, the company offered her the opportunity to buy company stock at a discount, and she received a number of bonuses that were paid in company stock. At the time, her company's stock was flying high, topped all of the must-have stock lists, and Megan felt lucky. She loved all of her years at the company, too. She had great memories and was dedicated to her company.

Thirty-four years later, even though she loved her job, Megan was ready to retire and spend more time with her grandchildren. She wasn't ready, however, to get rid of her company stock. By that time, she had amassed $300,000 in company stock, which made up a significant portion of her portfolio. Megan knew that holding that much in one stock wasn't wise, but though she didn't want to admit it, she was just too attached to her company to let it go. Soon, however, that stock began to lose value. Over the next ten years, the value dropped over and over. Each time, Megan told herself, "Buy low and sell high. Hang in there and it will rebound."

Megan is still hanging in there. She stuck with her automotive stock, even though it almost totally bottomed out. Today, things are looking up, but Megan is in her late 70s. When the stock price rises just a little bit more, she is planning to sell it to help pay for her grandkids' college. If only the stock price would rise just a little bit more...

THE IMPACT OF VOLATILITY ON THE INDIVIDUAL INVESTOR

In 2013, DALBAR, the well-respected financial services market research firm, released their annual "Quantitative Analysis of Investment Behavior" report (QAIB). The report studied the impact of market volatility on individual investors: a person like Lisa, or anyone who was managing (or mismanaging) their own investments in the stock market.

According to the study, volatility not only caused investors to make decisions based on their emotions, those decisions also harmed their investments and prevented them from realizing potential gains. So why do people meddle so much with their investments when the market is fluctuating? Part of the reason is that many people have financial obligations that they don't have control over. Significant expenses like house payments, the unexpected cost of replacing a broken-down car, and medical bills

AVOIDING EMOTIONAL INVESTING

can put people in a position where they need money. If they need to sell investments to come up with that money, they don't have the luxury of selling when they *want* to. They must sell when they *need* to.

DALBAR's "Quantitative Analysis of Investor Behavior" has been used to measure the effects of investors' buying, selling and mutual fund switching decisions since 1994. The QAIB shows time and time again over nearly a 20-year period that the average investor earns less, and in many cases, significantly less than the performance of mutual funds suggests. QAIB's goal is to improve independent investor performance and to help financial professionals provide helpful advice and investment strategies that address the concerns and behaviors of the average investor.

An excerpt from the report claims that:*

"QAIB offers guidance on how and where investor behaviors can be improved. No matter what the state of the mutual fund industry, boom or bust: Investment results are more dependent on investor behavior than on fund performance. Mutual fund investors who hold on to their investments are more successful than those who time the market.

QAIB uses data from the Investment Company Institute (ICI), Standard & Poor's and Barclays Capital Index Products to compare mutual fund investor returns to an appropriate set of benchmarks.

There are actually three primary causes for the chronic shortfall for both equity and fixed income investors:
1. *Capital not available to invest. This accounts for 25 percent to 35 percent of the shortfall.*
2. *Capital needed for other purposes. This accounts for 35 percent to 45 percent of the shortfall.*

---

*2013 QAIB, Dalbar, March 2013

3. *Psychological factors. These account for 45 percent to 55 percent of the shortfall."*

The key findings of Dalbar's QAIB report provide compelling statistics about how individual investment strategies produced negative outcomes for the majority of investors:
- Psychological factors account for 45 percent to 55 percent of the chronic investment return shortfall for both equity and fixed income investors.
- Asset allocation is designed to handle the investment decision-making for the investor, which can materially reduce the shortfall due to psychological factors.
- Successful asset allocation investing requires investors to act on two critical imperatives:
    1. Balance capital preservation and appreciation so that they are aligned with the investor's objective.
    2. Select a qualified allocator.
- The best way for an investor to determine their risk tolerance is to utilize a risk tolerance assessment. However, these assessments must be accessible and usable.
- Evaluating allocator quality requires analysis of the allocator's underlying investments, decision making process and whether or not past efforts have produced successful outcomes.
- Choosing a top allocator makes a significant difference in the investment results one will achieve.
- Mutual fund retention rates suggest that the average investor has not remained invested for long enough periods to derive the potential benefits of the investment markets.
- Retention rates for asset allocation funds exceed those of equity and fixed income funds by over a year.
- Investors' ability to correctly time the market is highly dependent on the direction of the market. Investors gen-

erally guess right more often in up markets. However, in 2012 investors guessed right only 42 percent of the time during a bull market.

- Analysis of investor fund flows compared to market performance further supports the argument that investors are unsuccessful at timing the market. Market upswings rarely coincide with mutual fund inflows while market downturns do not coincide with mutual fund outflows.
- Average equity mutual fund investors gained 15.56 percent compared to a gain of 15.98 percent that just holding the S&P 500 produced.
- The shortfall in the long-term annualized return of the average mutual fund equity investor and the S&P 500 continued to decrease in 2012.
- The fixed-income investor experienced a return of 4.68 percent compared to an advance of 4.21 percent on the Barclays Aggregate Bond Index.
- The average fixed income investor has failed to keep up with inflation in nine out of the last 14 years.*

It doesn't take a financial services market research report to tell you that market volatility is out of your control. The report does prove, however, that before you experience market volatility, you should have an investment plan, and when the market is fluctuating, you should stand by your investment plan. You should also review and discuss your investment plan with your financial professional on a regular basis, ensuring he/she is aware of any changes in your goals, financial circumstances, your health or your risk tolerance. When the economy is under stress and the markets are volatile, investors can feel vulnerable. That vulnerability causes people to tinker with their portfolios in an attempt to outsmart the market.

---

*2013 QAIB, Dalbar, March 2013

Financial professionals, however, don't try to time the market for their clients. They try to tap into the gains that can be realized by committing to long-term investment strategies.

CHAPTER 8 RECAP //
- Your money is personal, which makes emotional investing an almost unavoidable risk. That's a problem. As the 2013 DALBAR "Quantitative Analysis of Investment Behavior" report demonstrates, the average fixed income investor who makes investment decisions alone failed to keep up with inflation in nine out of the last 14 years.
- Seek the help of an investment expert in order to keep emotion out of your investing strategy. Financial professionals commit to proven and long-term investment strategies in order to help their clients achieve gains in the market.

9

THE MEANING OF YELLOW MONEY

"People who don't respect money don't have any."
– J. Paul Getty

Now that you've calculated the Rule of 100, determined how much risk you have and how much you want, and you've determined how much Green Money you need to meet your short-term and mid-term income needs, it's time to look at what you have left. The money you have left after you've calculated your Green Money needs has the potential of becoming Red Money: your stocks, mutual funds and other investment solutions that you want to continue accumulating value with the market. You now have the luxury of taking a closer second look at your Red Money to determine how you would like to manage it.

As you read earlier in the key findings of the DALBAR report, the deck is stacked against the individual investor. Remember that the average investor on a fixed income failed to keep pace with inflation in nine of the last 14 years, meaning the inherent risk in managing your Red Money is very real and could have a lasting impact on your assets.

So, how much of your Red Money do you invest, and in what kinds of markets, investment solutions and stocks do you invest? There are a lot of different directions in which you can take your Red Money. One thing is for sure: significant accumulation depends on investing in the market. How you go about doing it is different for everyone. Gathering stocks, bonds and investment funds together in a portfolio without a cohesive strategy behind them could cause you to miss out on the benefits of a more thoughtful and planful approach. The end result is that you may never really understand what your money is doing, where and how it is really invested, and which investment principles are behind the investment solutions you hold. While you may have goals for each individual piece of your portfolio, it is likely that you don't have a comprehensive plan for your Red Money, which may mean that *you are taking on more risk than you would like, and are getting less return for it than is possible.*

Enter **Yellow Money.** Yellow Money is money that is managed by a professional *with a purpose*. After your income needs are met and you have assets that you would like to dedicate to accumulation, there are decisions you need to make about how to invest those assets. You can buy stocks, index funds, mutual funds, bonds—you name it—you can invest in it. However, the difference between Red Money and Yellow Money is that Yellow Money has a cohesive strategy behind it that is *implemented by a professional*. When you manage your Red Money with an investment plan, it becomes Yellow Money: *money that is being managed with a specific purpose, a specific set of focused goals and a specific* *strategy in mind.* Yellow Money is still a type of Red Money. It comes with different levels of risk. But Yellow Money is under the watchful eye of professionals who have a stake in the success of your money in the market and who can recommend a range of strategies from those designed for preservation to those targeting rapid growth. You don't want to miss out on achieving the right level of risk, and more importantly, composing a careful plan for the return of your assets.

It can be helpful to think of Red Money and Yellow Money with this analogy:

If you needed to travel through an unfamiliar city in a foreign country, you could rent a car or perhaps hire a driver. Were you to drive yourself, you would try to gain guidance from perplexing road signs and need to adhere to traffic rules—with no experience or assistance to lean on. It would take longer to get to where you want to go, and the chance of a traffic accident would be higher. If you hired a driver, they would manage your journey. A driver would know the route, how to avoid traffic, and follow the rules of the road.

Red Money is like driving yourself. With Yellow Money, you are still traveling by car, but now you have a professional working on your behalf.

TAKING A CLOSER LOOK AT YOUR PORTFOLIO

Think about your investment portfolio. Think specifically of what you would consider your Red Money. Do you know what is there? You may have several different investment solutions like individual mutual funds, bond accounts, stocks, etc. You may have inherited a stock portfolio from a relative, or you might be invested in a bond account offered by the company for which you worked due to your familiarity with them. While you may or may not be managing your investments individually, the reality is that you probably don't have an overall management strategy for all of your investments. Investments that aren't managed are simply Red Money, or money that is at risk in the market.

Harnessing the earning potential of your Red Money relies on more than a collection of stocks and bonds, however. It needs guided management. A good Yellow Money manager uses the knowledge they have about the level of risk with which you are comfortable, what you need or want to use your money for, when you want or need it and how you want to use it. The Yellow Money objects that they choose for you will still have a certain level of risk, but under the right management, control and process, you have a far better chance of a successful outcome that meets your specific needs.

When you sit down with an investment professional, you can look at all of your assets together. Chances are that you have accumulated a number of different assets over the last 20, 30 or 50 years. You may have a 401(k), an IRA, a Roth IRA, an account of self-directed stocks, a brokerage account, etc. Wherever you put your money, a financial professional will go through your assets and help you determine the level of risk to which you are exposed now and should be exposed in the future.

Here is a typical example of how an investment professional can be helpful to a future retiree with Yellow Money needs:

> » *Janet is 65 years old and wants to retire in two years. She has a 401(k) from her job to which she has contributed for 26 years. She also has some stocks that her late husband managed. Janet also has $55,000 in a mutual fund that her sister recommended to her five years ago and $30,000 in another mutual fund that she heard about at work. She takes a look at her assets one day and decides that she doesn't understand what they add up to or what kind of retirement they will provide. She decides to meet with an investment professional. Janet's professional immediately asks her:*

1. Does she know exactly where all of her money is? *Janet doesn't know much about all her husband's stocks, which have now become hers. Their value is at $100,000 invested in three large cap companies. Janet is unsure of the companies and whether she should hold or sell them.*

2. Does she know what types of assets she owns? *Yes and no. She knows she had a 401(k) and IRAs, but she is unfamiliar with her husband's self-directed stock portfolio or the type of mutual funds she owns. Furthermore she is unclear as to how to manage the holdings as she nears retirement.*

3. Does she know the strategies behind each one of the investment solutions she owns? *While Janet knows she had a 401(k), an IRA and mutual fund holdings, she doesn't know how her 401(k) is organized or how to make it more conservative as she nears retirement. She is unsure whether her IRA is a Roth or traditional variety and how to draw income from them? She really does not have specific investment principles guiding her investment decisions, and she doesn't know anything about her husband's individual stocks. One major concern for Janet is whether her family would be okay if she were not around?*

After determining Janet's assets, her financial professional prepares a consolidated report that lays out all of her assets for her to review. Her professional explains each one of them to her. Janet discovers that although she is two years away from retiring, her 401(k) is organized with an amount of risk with which she is not comfortable. Sixty percent of her 401(k) is at risk, far off the mark if we abide by the Rule of 100. Janet opts to be more conservative than the Rule of 100 suggests, as she will rely on her 401(k) for most of her immediate income needs after retirement. Janet's professional also points out several instances of overlap between her mutual funds. Janet learns that while she is comfortable with one of her mutual funds, she does not agree with the management principles of the other. In the end, Janet's professional helps her re-organize her 401(k) to secure her more Green Money for retirement income. Her professional also uses her mutual fund and her husband's stock assets to create a growth oriented investment plan that Janet will rely on for Need Later Money in 15 years when she plans on relocating closer to her children and grandchildren. By creating an overall investment strategy, Janet is able to meet her targeted goals in retirement. Janet's financial professional worked closely with her and her tax professional to minimize the tax impact of any asset sales on Janet's situation.

Like Janet, you may have several savings vehicles: a 401(k), an IRA to which you regularly contribute, some mutual funds to which you make monthly contributions, etc. But what is your *overall investment strategy?* Do you have one in place? Do you want one that will help you meet your retirement goals? Yellow Money looks at ALL your accounts and all their different strategies to create a plan that helps them all work together. Your current investment situation may not reflect your wishes. As a matter of fact, it likely doesn't.

You may have a better understanding of your assets than Janet did, but even someone with an investment strategy can benefit from having a financial professional review their portfolio:

» *Charles is 69 years old. He retired four years ago. He relied on income from an IRA for three years in order to increase his Social Security benefit. He also made significant investments in 36 different mutual funds. He chose to diversify among the funds by selecting a portion for growth, another for good dividends, another that focused on promising small cap companies and a final portion that work like index funds. All the* money that Charles had in mutual funds he considered Need Later Money that he wanted to rely on in his 80s. *After the stock market took a hit in 2008, Charles lost some confidence in his investments and decided to sit down with a financial professional to see if his portfolio was able to recover.*

The professional Charles met with was able to determine what goals he had in mind. Specifically, the financial professional determined what Charles actually wanted and needed the money for, and when he needed it. His professional also looked inside each of the mutual funds and discovered several instances of overlap. While Charles had created diversity in his portfolio by selecting funds focused on different goals, he didn't account for overlap in the companies in which the funds were invested. Out of the 36 funds, his professional found that 20 owned nearly identical stock. While most of the companies were good investments, the high instance of overlap did not contribute to the healthy investment diversity that Charles wanted. Charles's financial professional also provided him with a report that explained the concentration ratio of his holdings (noting how much of his portfolio was contained within the top 25 stock holdings), the percentage of his portfolio that each company in which he invested in represented (showing the percentage of net assets that each company made up as an overall position in his portfolio) and the portfolio date of his account (showing when the funds in his portfolio were last updated: as funds are required to report updates only twice per year, it was possible that some of his fund reports could be six months old).

Charles's professional consolidated his assets into one investment management strategy. This allowed Charles's investments to be managed by someone he trusted who knew his specific investment goals and needs. Eliminating redundancy and overlap in his portfolio was easy to do but difficult to detect since Charles had multiple funds with multiple brokerage firms. Charles sat down with a professional to see if his mutual funds could perform well, and he left with a consolidated management plan and a money manager that understood him personally. That's Yellow Money at its best.

AVOIDING EMOTIONAL INVESTING

There's no way around it; people get emotional about their money. And for good reason. You've spent your life working for it, exchanging your time and talent for it, and making decisions about how to invest it, save it and make it grow. The maintenance of your lifestyle and your plans for retirement all depend on it. The best investment strategies, however, don't rely on emotions. One of Yellow Money's greatest strengths lies in the fact that it is managed by someone who understands your needs and desires, but doesn't make decisions about your money under the influence of emotion.

A well-managed investment account meets your goals as a whole, not in individualized and piecemeal ways. Professional money managers do this by creating requirements for each type of investment in which they put your money. We'll call them "screens." Your money manager will run your holdings through the screens they have created to evaluate different types of investment strategies. A professionally managed account will only have holdings that meet the requirements laid out in the overall management plan that was designed to meet your investment goals. The holdings that don't make it through the screens, the ones that don't contribute to your investment goals, are sold and redistributed to investments that your financial professional has determined to be appropriate.

Different screens apply to different Yellow Money strategies. For example, if one of your goals is significant growth, which would require taking on more risk alongside the potential for more return, an investment professional would screen for companies that have high rates of revenue and sales growth, high earnings growth, rising profit margins, and innovative solutions. On the other hand, if you want your portfolio to be used for income, which would call for lower risk and less return, your professional would screen for dividend yield and sector diversification. *Every investor has a different goal, and every goal requires a customized strategy that uses quantitative screens.* A professional will create a portfolio that reflects your investment desires. If some of the current assets you own complement the strategies that your professional recommends, those will likely stay in your portfolio.

Screening your assets removes emotions from the equation. It removes attachment to underperforming or overly risky investments. Financial professionals aren't married to particular stocks or mutual funds for any reason. They go by the numbers and see your portfolio through a lens shaped by your retirement goals. Your professional understands your wants and needs, and creates an investment strategy that takes your life events and future plans into account. It's a planful approach, and it allows you to tap into the tools and resources of a professional who has built a career around successful investing. Managing money is a full time job and is best left to a professional money manager.

Removing emotions from investing also allows you to be unaffected by the day-to-day volatility of the market. Your financial professional doesn't ask where the market is going to be in a year, three years or a month from now. If you look at the value of the stock market from the beginning of the twentieth century to today, it's going up. Despite the Great Depression, despite the 1987 crash, despite the 2008 market downturn, the market, as a whole, trends up. Remember the major market downturn in 2008 when the market lost 30 percent of its value? Not only did it completely recover, it has far exceeded its 2008 value. Emotional investing led countless people to sell low as the market went down, and buy the same shares back when the market started to recover. That's an expensive way to do business. While you can't afford to lose money that you need in two, three or five years, your Need Later Money has time to grow. The best way to do so is to make it Yellow.

CREATING AN INVESTMENT STRATEGY

Just like Janet and Charles, chances are that you can benefit from taking a more managed investment approach tailored to your goals. Yellow Money is generally Need Later Money that you want to grow for needs you'll have in at least 10 years. You can work with your financial planner to create investments that meet your needs within different timeframes. You may need to rely on some of your Yellow Money in 10, 15 or 20 years, whether for additional income, a large purchase you plan on making or a vacation. Whatever you want it for, you will need it down the road. A financial professional can help you re-scale the risk of your assets as they grow, helping you lock in your profits and secure a source of income you can depend on later.

So what does a Yellow Money account look like? Here's what it *doesn't* look like: a portfolio with 49 small cap mutual funds, a dozen individual stocks and an assortment of bond accounts. A brokerage account with a hodgepodge of investments, even if goal-oriented, is not a professionally managed account. It's still Red Money. Remember, Yellow Money is a managed account that has an overarching investment philosophy. When you look at making investments that will perform to meet your future income needs, the burning question becomes: How much should you have in the market and how should it be invested? Working with a professional will help you determine how much risk you should take, how to balance your assets so they will meet your goals and how to plan for the big ticket items, like health care expenses, that may be in your future. Yes, Yellow Money is exposed to risk, but by working with a professional, you can manage that risk in a productive way.

WHY YELLOW MONEY?

If you have met your immediate income needs for retirement, why bother with professionally managing your other assets? The money you have accumulated above and beyond your income needs probably has a greater purpose. It may be for your children or grandchildren. You may want to give money to a charity or organization that you admire. In short, you may want to craft your legacy. It would be advantageous to grow your assets in the best manner possible. A financial professional has built a career around managing money in profitable ways. They are experts under the supervision of the organization that they represent.

Turning to Yellow Money also means that you don't have to burden yourself with the time commitment, the stress, and the cost of determining how to manage your money. Yellow Money can help you better enjoy your retirement. Do you want to sit down in your home office every day and determine how to best allocate your assets, or do you want to be living your life while someone else manages your money for you? When a financial professional manages the majority of your Red Money with a specific purpose, you don't have to be worrying about which stocks to buy and sell today or tomorrow.

SEEKING FINANCIAL ADVICE: STOCK BROKERS VS. INVESTMENT ADVISOR REPRESENTATIVES

Investors basically have access to two types of advice in today's financial world: advice from stockbrokers and advice given by investment advisors. Most investors, however, don't know the difference between types of advice and the people from whom they receive advice. Today, there are two primary types of advice offered to investors: advice given by a commission-based registered

representative (brokers) and advice given by fee-based Investment Advisor Representatives. Unfortunately, many investors are not aware that a difference exists; nor have they been explained the distinction between the two types of advice. In a survey taken by TD Ameritrade, the top reasons investors choose to work with an independent registered investment advisor are:*
- Registered Investment Advisors are required, as fiduciaries, to offer advice that is in the best interest of clients
- More personalized service and competitive fee structure offered at a Registered Investment Advisor firm
- Dissatisfaction with full commission brokers

The truth is that there is a great deal of difference between stockbrokers and investment advisor representatives. For starters, investment advisor representatives are obligated to act in an investor's best interests in every and all aspect of a financial relationship. Confusion continues to exist among investors struggling to find the best financial advice out there and the most credible sources of advice.

Here is some information to help clear up the confusion so you can find good advice from a professional you can trust:
- Investment advisor representatives have the fiduciary duty to act in a client's best interest at all times with every investment decision they make. Stockbrokers and brokerage firms usually do not act as fiduciaries to their investors and are not obligated to make decisions that are entirely in the best interest of their customers. For example, if you decide you want to invest in precious metals, a stockbroker would offer you a precious metals account from their firm. An Investment Advisor would find you a precious

---

*2011 Advisor Sentiment Study, commissioned by TD AMERITRADE. TD Ameritrade, Inc.

metals account that is the best fit for you based on the investment strategy of your portfolio.
- Investment advisors give their clients a Form ADV describing the methods that the professional uses to do business. An Investment Advisor also obtains client consent regarding any conflicts of interest that could exist with the business of the professional.
- Stockbrokers and brokerage firms are not obligated to provide comparable types of disclosure to their customers.
- Whereas stockbrokers and firms routinely earn large profits by trading as principal with customers, Investment Advisors cannot trade with clients as principal (except in very limited and specific circumstances).
- Investment Advisors charge a pre-negotiated fee with their clients in advance of any transactions. They cannot earn additional profits or commissions from their customers' investments without prior consent. Registered Investment Advisors are commonly paid an asset-based fee that aligns their interests with those of their clients. Brokerage firms and stockbrokers, on the other hand, have much different payment agreements. Their revenues may increase regardless of the performance of their customers' assets.
- Unlike brokerage firms, where investment banking and underwriting are commonplace, Registered Investment Advisors must manage money in the best interests of their customers. Because Registered Investment Advisors charge set fees for their services, their focus is on their client. Brokerage firms may focus on other aspects of the firm that do not contribute to the improvement of their clients' assets.
- Unlike brokers, Registered Investment Advisors typically do not get commissions from fund or insurance companies for selling their investment solutions.

Just to drive home the point, here is what a fiduciary duty to a client means for a Registered Investment Advisor. Registered Investment Advisors must:*

- Always act in the best interest of their client and make investment decisions that reflect their goals.
- Identify and monitor securities that are illiquid.
- When appropriate, employ fair market valuation procedures.
- Observe procedures regarding the allocation of investment opportunities, including new issues and the aggregation of orders.
- Have policies regarding affiliated broker-dealers and maintenance of brokerage accounts.
- Disclose all conflicts of interest.
- Have policies on use of brokerage commissions for research.
- Have policies regarding directed brokerage, including step-out trades and payment for order flow.
- Abide by a code of ethics.

---

*2011 Advisor Sentiment Study, commissioned by TD AMERITRADE. TD Ameritrade, Inc.

CHAPTER 9 RECAP //
- Yellow Money may make Red Money less dangerous.
- Yellow Money is professionally managed.
- Yellow Money has a cohesive purpose and a strategy behind it.
- If you haven't sat down and thought about how much money you need in order to generate income during retirement, you're just speculating.
- Red Money is like driving yourself in unfamiliar territory. With Yellow Money, you are still traveling by car, but now you have a professional driving on your behalf.
- The deck is stacked against the ordinary investor. According to the DALBAR report, individual investors consistently underperform compared to the market because of a variety of factors, including emotional investing.
- Yellow Money is managed without emotions.
- Checking your truly Red Money should be like checking the sports section. You are interested in it, but it won't directly affect your lifestyle. If your Red Money goes down 50 percent, no one should have to scrape you off the floor.

10
UNDERSTANDING NEW IDEAS FOR INVESTING

"If you have trouble imagining a 20 percent loss in the stock market, you shouldn't be in stocks."
– John Bogle

In Chapter 1, we discussed how today's investment options require advice that is relevant to today. Traditional, outdated investment strategies are not only ineffective, they can be harmful to the average investor. One of the most traditional ways of thinking about investing is the risk versus reward trade-off. It goes something like this.

Investment options that are considered safer carry less risk, but also offer the potential for less return. Riskier investment options carry the burden of volatility and a greater potential for loss, but they also offer a greater potential for large rewards. Most professionals move their clients back and forth along this range, shifting between investments that are safer and investments that are structured for growth. Essentially, the old rules of investing dictate that you can either choose relative safety *or* return, but you can't have both.

Updated investment strategies work with the flexibility of liquidity to remake the rules. Here is how:

There are three dimensions that are inherent in any investment: *Liquidity, Safety,* and *Return.* You can maximize any two of these dimensions at the expense of the third. If you choose Safety and Liquidity, this is like keeping your assets in a checking account or savings account. This option delivers a lot of Safety and Liquidity, but at the expense of any Return. On the other hand, if you choose Liquidity and Return, meaning you have the potential for great return and can still reclaim your money whenever you choose, you will likely be exposed to a very high level of risk.

Understanding Liquidity can help you break the old Risk versus Safety trade-off. By identifying assets from which you don't require Liquidity, you can place yourself in a position to potentially profit from relatively safe investments that provide a higher than average rate of return.

Choosing Safety and Return over Liquidity can have significant impacts on the accumulation of your assets. In Ted's case, the paradigm shift from earning and saving to leveraging assets was a costly one.

> » *Ted is a corn and soybean farmer with 1,200 acres of land. He routinely retains somewhere between $40,000 and $80,000 in his checking and savings accounts. If a major piece of equipment fails and needs repair or replacement, Ted will need the money available to pay for the equipment and carry on with farming. If the price of feed for his cattle goes up one year, he will need to compensate for the increased*

overhead to his farming operation. He isn't a particularly wealthy farmer, but he has little choice but to keep a portion of money on hand in case something comes up and he must access it quickly. Most of his capital is held in livestock in the pasture or crops in the ground tied up for six to eight months of the year. When a major financial need arises, Ted can't just harvest 10 acres of soybeans and use them for payment. He needs to depend heavily on Liquidity in order to be a successful farmer.

Old habits die hard, however, and when Ted finally hangs up his overalls and quits farming, he keeps his bank accounts flush with cash, just like in the old days. After selling the farm and the equipment, Ted keeps a huge portion of the profits in Liquid investments because that's what he is familiar with. Unfortunately for Ted, with his pile of money sitting in his checking account, he isn't even keeping pace with inflation. After all his hard work as a farmer, his money is losing value every day. Perhaps shifting to a paradigm of leveraging assets to potentially generate income and accumulate value may have been a better alternative.

Almost anything would be a better option for Ted than clinging to Liquidity. He could have done something better to get either more return from his money or more safety, and at the very least would not have lost out to inflation.

As you can see, choosing Liquidity solely can be a costly option. The sooner you want your money back, the less you can leverage it for Safety or Return. If you have the option of putting your money in a long-term investment, you will be sacrificing Liquidity, but potentially gaining both Safety and Return. Rethinking your approach to money in this way can make a world of difference and can provide you with a structured way to generate income while allowing the value of your asset to grow over time.

The question is, how much Liquidity do you *really* need? Think about it. If you haven't sat down and created an income plan for your retirement, your perceived need for Liquidity is a guess. You don't know how much cash you'll need to fill the income gap if you don't know the amount of your Social Security benefit of the total of your other income options. If you *have* determined your income need and have made a plan for filling your income gap, you can partition your assets based on when you will need them. With an income plan in place, *you can use new rules to enjoy both Safety and Return from your assets.*

CHAPTER 10 RECAP //

- Investment Advisors are obligated to make investment decisions or recommendations that are in your best interests and are aligned with your financial situation, timeframe and risk tolerance, and to put your interests ahead of their own. Stockbrokers and brokerage firms are obligated to make suitable recommendations from the universe of products they are permitted to sell.

11
PAYING TAXES AS A RETIREE

"The problem is not that people are taxed too little; the problem is that the government spends too much."
— Ronald Reagan

Taxes play a starring role in the theater of retirement planning. Unfortunately, many people approach taxes the wrong way. If you've been working with a CPA to record everything you earned and spent the previous year, and then figure out how much you owe in taxes, what you've been doing is tax reporting. If you've been working with a CPA to create a strategy for what you will spend, where you'll get that money and how your actions will affect your taxes, that's called tax planning. Tax planning is a great strategy, particularly for retirees. It can help you keep more of the income you worked hard to earn and save, as well as protect your assets and your legacy.

Tax planning is not only for the wealthy. You can benefit tremendously from working with a professional qualified to help make sure you are not paying too much in taxes year after year. A qualified professional can also implement long-term tax strategies that will help preserve everything you've worked so hard to build.

TAXES AND RETIREMENT

When you retire, you move from the earning and accumulation phase of your life into the asset distribution phase of your life. For most people, that means relying on Social Security, a 401(k), an IRA, or a pension. Wherever you have put your Green Money for retirement, you are going to start relying on it to provide you with the income that once came as a paycheck. Most of these distributions will be considered income by the IRS and will be taxed as such. There are exceptions to that (not all of your Social Security income is taxed, and income from Roth IRAs is not taxed), but for the most part, your distributions will be subject to income taxes.

Regarding assets that you have in an IRA or a 401(k) plan that uses an IRA, when you reach 70 ½ years of age, you will be required to draw a certain amount of money from your IRA as income each year. That amount depends on your age and the balance in your IRA. The amount that you are required to withdraw as income is called a Required Minimum Distribution (RMD). Why are you required to withdraw money from your own account? Chances are the money in that account has grown over time, and the government wants to collect taxes on that growth. If you have a large balance in an IRA, there's a chance your RMD could increase your income significantly enough to put you into a higher tax bracket, subjecting you to a higher tax rate.

Here's where tax planning can really begin to work strongly in your favor. In the distribution phase of your life, you have a predictable income based on your RMDs, your Social Security benefit and any other income-generating assets you may have. What really impacts you at this stage is how much of that money you keep in your pocket after taxes. Essentially, *you will make more money saving on taxes than you will by making more money.* If you can reduce your tax burden by 30, 20 or even 10 percent, you earn yourself that much more money by not paying it in taxes.

How do you save money on taxes? By having a plan. In this instance, a financial professional can work with the CPAs at their firm to create a **distribution plan** that minimizes your taxes and maximizes your annual net income.

BUILDING A TAX DIVERSIFIED PORTFOLIO

So far so good: avoid taxes, maximize your net annual income and have a plan for doing it. When people decide to leverage the experience and resources of a financial professional, they may not be thinking of how distribution planning and tax planning will benefit their portfolios. Often more exciting prospects like planning income annuities, investing in the market and structuring investments for growth rule the day. Taxes, however, play a crucial role in retirement planning. Achieving those tax goals requires knowledge of options, foresight and professional guidance.

Finding the path to a good tax plan isn't always a simple task. Every tax return you file is different from the one before it because things constantly change. Your expenses change. Planned or unplanned purchases occur. Health care costs, medical bills, an inheritance, property purchases, reaching an age where your RMD kicks in or travel, any number of things can affect how much income you report and how many deductions you take each year.

Preparing for the ever-changing landscape of your financial life requires a tax-diversified portfolio that can be leveraged to balance the incomes, expenditures and deductions that affect you each year. A financial professional will work with you to answer questions like these:

What does your tax landscape look like?

- Do you have a tax-diversified portfolio robust enough to adapt to your needs?
- Do you have a diversity of taxable and non-taxable income planned for your retirement?
- Will you be able to maximize your distributions to take advantage of your deductions when you retire?
- Is your portfolio strong enough and tax-diversified enough to adapt to an ever-changing (and usually increasing) tax code?

» When Darlene returns home after a week in the hospital recovering from a knee replacement, the 77-year-old calls her daughter, sister and brother to let them know she is home and feeling well. She also should have called her CPA. Darlene's medical expenses for the procedure, her hospital stay, her medications and the ongoing physical therapy she attended amount to more than $50,000.

Currently, Americans can deduct medical expenses that are more than 10 percent of their Adjusted Gross Income (AGI). Darlene's AGI is $60,000 the year of her knee replacement, meaning she is able to deduct $45,500 of her medical bills from her taxes that year. Her AGI dictated that she could deduct more than 80 percent of her medical expenses that year. **Darlene didn't know this.**

Had she been working with a financial professional who regularly asked her about any changes in her life, her spending, or her expenses (expected or unexpected), Darlene

could have saved thousands of dollars. Darlene can also file an amendment to her tax return to recoup the overpayment.
This scenario presumes permanent laws in effect subsequent to 12/31/16

This relatively simple example of how tax planning can save you money is just the tip of the iceberg. No one can be expected to know the entire U.S. tax code. But a professional who is working with a team of CPAs and financial professionals have an advantage over the average taxpayer who must start from square one on their own every year. Have you been taking advantage of all the deductions that are available to you?

PROACTIVE TAX PLANNING
The implications of proactive tax planning are far reaching, and are larger than many people realize. Remember, doing your taxes in January, February, March or April means you are writing a history book. Planning your taxes in October, November or December means that you are writing the story as it happens. You can look at all the factors that are at play and make decisions that will impact your tax return *before* you file it.

Realizing that tax planning is an aspect of financial planning is an important leap to make. When you incorporate tax planning into your financial planning strategy, it becomes part of the way you maximize your financial potential. Paying less in taxes means you keep more of your money. Simply put, the more money you keep, the more of it you can leverage as an asset. This kind of planning can affect you at any stage of your life. If you are 40 years old, are you contributing the maximum amount to your 401(k) plan? Are you contributing to a Roth IRA? Are you finding ways to structure the savings you are dedicating to your children's education? Do you have life insurance? Taxes and tax planning affects all of these investment tools. Having a relationship with a professional who works with a CPA can help you build a truly comprehensive financial plan that not only works with your investments, but also shapes your assets to find the most efficient ways to prepare for tax time. There may be years that you could benefit from higher distributions because of the tax bracket that you are in, or there could be years you would benefit from taking less. There may be years when you have a lot of deductions and years you have relatively few. **Adapting your distributions to work in concert with your available deductions** is at the heart of smart tax planning. Professional guidance can bring you to the next level of income distribution, allowing you to remain flexible enough to maximize your tax efficiency. And remember, saving money on taxes makes you more money than making money does.

What you have on paper is important: your assets, savings, investments, which are financial expression of your work and time. It's just as important to know how to get it off the paper in a way that keeps most of it in your pocket. Almost anything that involves financial planning also involves taxes. Annuities, investments, IRAs, 401(k)s, 403(b), and many other investment options will have tax implications. Life also has a way of throwing curveballs. Illness, expensive car repair or replacement, or *any event that has a financial impact on your life will likely have a corresponding tax implication* around which you should adapt your financial plan. Tax planning does just that.

One dollar can end up being less than 25 cents to your heirs.

> » *When Peter's father passed away, he discovered that he was the beneficiary of his father's $500,000 IRA. Peter has a wife and a family of four children, and he knew that his father had intended for a large portion of the IRA to go toward funding their college educations.*

PAYING TAXES AS A RETIREE

After Peter's father's estate is distributed, Peter, who is 50 years old and whose two oldest sons are entering college, liquidates the IRA. By doing so, his taxable income for that year puts him in a 39.6 percent tax bracket, immediately reducing the value of the asset to $302,000. An additional 3.8 percent surtax on net investment income further diminishes the funds to $283,000. Liquidating the IRA in effect subjects much of Peter's regular income to the surtax, as well. At this point, Peter will be taxed at 43.4 percent.

Peter's state taxes are an additional 9 percent. Moreover, estate taxes on Peter's father's assets claim another 22 percent. By the time the IRS is through, Peter's income from the IRA will be taxed at 75 percent, leaving him with $125,000 of the original $500,000. While it would help contribute to the education of his children, it wouldn't come anywhere near completely paying for it, something the $500,000 could have easily done.

As the above example makes clear, leaving an asset to your beneficiaries can be more complicated than it may seem. In the case of a traditional IRA, after federal, estate and state taxes, the asset could literally diminish to as little as 25 percent of its value.

How does working with a professional help you make smarter tax decisions with your own finances? Any financial professional worth their salt will be working with a firm that has a team of trained tax professionals, including CPAs, who have an intimate knowledge of the tax code and how to adapt a financial plan to it.

Here's another example of how taxes have major implications on asset management:

» *Greg and Rhonda, a 62-year-old couple, begin working with a financial professional in October. After structuring their assets to reflect their risk tolerance and creating assets that would provide them Green Money income during retirement, they feel good about their situation. They make decisions that allow them to maximize their Social Security benefits, they have plenty of options for filling their income gap, and have begun a safe yet ambitious Yellow Money strategy with their professional. When their professional asks them about their tax plan, they tell him their CPA handled their taxes every year, and did a great job. Their professional says, "I don't mean who does your taxes, I mean, who does your tax planning?" Greg and Rhonda aren't sure how to respond.*

Their professional brings Greg and Rhonda's financial plan to the firm's CPA and has her run a tax projection for them. A week later their professional calls them with a tax plan for the year that will save them more than $3,000 on their tax return. The couple is shocked. A simple piece of advice from the CPA based on the numbers revealed that if they paid their estimated taxes before the end of the year, they would be able to itemize it as a deduction, allowing them to save thousands of dollars.

This solution won't work for everyone, and it may not work for Greg and Rhonda every year. That's not the point. By being proactive with their approach to taxes and using the resources made available by their financial professional, they were able to create a tax plan that saved them money.

YELLOW MONEY AND TAXES

There are also tax implications for the money that you have managed professionally. People with portions of their investment portfolio that are actively traded can particularly benefit from having a proactive tax strategy. Without going into too much detail, for tax purposes there are two kinds of investment money: qualified and non-qualified. Different investment strategies can have different

PAYING TAXES AS A RETIREE

effects on how you are taxed on your investments and the growth of your investments. Some are more beneficial for one kind of investment strategy over another. Determining how to plan for the taxation of non-qualified and qualified investments is fodder for holiday party discussions at accounting firms. While it may not be a stimulating topic for the average investor, you don't have to understand exactly how it works in order to benefit from it.

While there are many differences between qualified and non-qualified investments, the main difference is this: qualified plans are designed to give investors tax benefits by deferring taxation of their growth until they are withdrawn. Non-qualified investments are not eligible for these deferral benefits. As such, non-qualified investments are taxed whenever income is realized from them in the form of growth.

Actively and non-actively traded investments provide a simple example of how to position your investments for the best tax advantage. In an actively traded and managed portfolio, there is a high amount of buying and selling of stocks, bonds, funds, ETFs, etc. If that active portfolio of non-qualified investments does well and makes a 20 percent return one year and you are in the 39.6 percent tax bracket, your net gain from that portfolio is only about 12 percent (39.6 percent tax of the 20 percent gain is roughly 8 percent.) In a passive trading strategy, you can use a qualified investment tool, such as an IRA, to achieve 13, 14 or 15 percent growth (much lower than the actively traded portfolio), but still realize a higher net return because the growth of the qualified investment is not taxed until it is withdrawn.

Does this mean that you have to always rely on a buy and hold strategy in qualified investment tools? Not necessarily. The question is, if you have qualified and non-qualified investments, where do you want to position your actively traded and managed assets? Incorporating a planful approach to positioning your investments for more beneficial taxation can be done many ways, but let's consider one example. Keeping your actively managed investment strategies inside an IRA or some other qualified plan could allow you to realize the higher gains of those investments without paying tax on their growth every year. Your more passively managed funds could then be kept in taxable, non-qualified vehicles and methods, and because you aren't realizing income from them on an annual basis by frequently trading them, they grow sheltered from taxation.

If you are interested in taking advantage of tax strategies that maximize your net income, you need the attentive strategies, experience and knowledge of a professional who can give you options that position you for profit. At the end of the day, what's important to you as the consumer is how much you keep, your after-tax take home.

ESTATE TAXES

The government doesn't just tax your income from investments while you're alive. They will also dip into your legacy.

While estate taxes aren't as hot of a topic as they were a few years ago, they are still an issue of concern for many people with assets. While taxes may not apply on estates that are less than $5 million, certain states have estate taxes with much lower exclusion ratios. Some are as low as $600,000. Many people may have to pay a state estate tax. One strategy for avoiding those types of taxes is to move assets outside of your estate. That can include gifting them to family or friends, or putting them into an irrevocable trust. Life insurance is another option for protecting your legacy.

CHAPTER 11 RECAP //

- There is a big difference between tax reporting and tax planning. Retirees can protect their assets, keep more of their income and preserve their legacies by planning their taxes with a qualified professional.
- Before you make major financial decisions, consult your financial and/or tax professional. It's not uncommon for retirees to accidentally trigger unnecessary and detrimental tax events because of a lack of planning.
- Always remember the RMD: when you reach the age of 70 ½, if you are a traditional IRA participant, the federal government requires you to take an RMD, or Required Minimum Distribution. Failure to take your RMD can be one of the most damaging retirement mistakes, costing you thousands of dollars in taxes and penalty fees.

STRATEGIC WEALTH: A TACTICAL AND PRACTICAL
GUIDE TO WINNING IN RETIREMENT

12
LOOKING INTO YOUR TAX FUTURE

"The hardest thing in the world to understand is the income tax."
— Albert Einstein

Tax legislation over the course of American history has left one very resounding message: taxes go up. Sadly, we hear this same threat so often that it has begun to sound like the boy who cried wolf. The reason behind this lies in the fact that tax hikes usually do not take effect until two or three years after their introduction and subsequently get piecemeal implementation. The result of this prolonged implementation period can be equated to death by a thousand paper cuts.

DEBT CEILING – CAUSE AND EFFECTS

The raising of the debt ceiling raised more than just the ability for our government to go further into debt. It also raised concerns and fears about the future of our economy. We are now seeing major swings in the markets with investors showing serious concerns over the future of investment valuations and their personal wealth. Unfortunately, the reasoning behind all of this uncertainty is preceded by the inability to see the full implications of what is in store. We rarely talk about the fact that the discussions on raising the debt ceiling were coupled to discussions on major tax reforms needed to correct the problems underlining the debt ceiling increase itself.

Increasing the debt ceiling was needed because the government maxed out its credit card, so to speak, which it has been living off of for quite some time. It is really not much different than what we have been seeing from the general public for the past few decades. Unfortunately, most of us do not have the ability to get a credit limit increase on our credit cards once we reach the maximum limit, that is unless we can show the ability to pay this balance back. The only way to pay this credit card back is by spending less and making more money.

This is exactly where the federal government is today. They have been given a higher credit limit, but they still must find a way to decrease the spending while making more money. The only way the government makes money is by collecting taxes.

Unfortunately, at the current moment, the government is collecting approximately $120 billion less per month than it currently spends. Discussions for major tax reform have accompanied the discussions for the increased debt ceiling.

DEBT AND EARNINGS

Let us take a closer look at where we are today. The U.S. national debt is increasing at an alarming rate, rising to levels never seen before and threatening serious harm to the economy. Through the end of 2010, the national debt has risen to $13.6 trillion, averaging an 11.4 percent increase annually over the past five years and a 9.2 percent increase annually over the past 10 years. To put this into perspective, the national gross domestic product (GDP) has increased to $14.5 trillion during the same period, averaging a 2.9 percent annual increase over the past five years and a 3.9 percent increase over the past 10 years. At the end of 2010, the national debt level was 93 percent of the GDP. Economists believe that a sustainable economy exists at a maximum level of approximately 80 percent. As of December 20, 2013, the U.S. national debt is 107.69 percent of GDP with the debt at $17.252 trillion and the GDP at $16.020 trillion.*

The significance of these two numbers lies within the contrast. The national debt is the amount that needs to be repaid. This is the credit card balance. Gross domestic product on the other hand is less known and represents the market value of all final goods and services produced within a country during a given period. Essentially, GDP represents the gross taxable income available to the government. If debts are increasing at a greater rate than the gross income available for taxation, then the only way to make up the difference is by increasing the rate at which the gross income is taxed.

The most recent presidential budget shows a continuing trend in the disparity between growth in the national debt and GDP over the next two decades. Although the increasing disparity is a real concern and shows that, at least in the short run, the federal deficit will not be addressed to counteract the potential crisis ahead, it is the revenue collection that tells the disconcerting story. Over the past 40 years the average collection of GDP has

---

* *http://www.usdebtclock.org/12/20/13*

been approximately 17.6 percent and currently collections are at approximately 14.4 percent of GDP.

As the presidential budget reveals, the projected revenues are estimated to be 20 percent by the end of the next decade. That is a 38.8 percent increase from the current tax levels. To put this into perspective, if you are currently in the top tax bracket of 35 percent and this bracket increases by the proposed collection increase, your tax rate will be approximately 48.5 percent. Keep in mind that even at this rate the deficit is projected to increase.

2013 – THE END OF AN ERA?

From a historical point of view, taxes are extremely low. The last time the U.S. national debt was at the same percentage level of GDP as today was at the end of World War II and several years following. The maximum tax rate averaged 90 percent from 1944 through 1963. Compare that to the maximum rate of 35 percent today and it becomes very clear that there is a disparity of extreme proportion.

Taxes during this historical period were at extreme levels for nearly 20 years, during and following this current level of debt-to-GDP. A significant point to note about the difference between that time and today is the economic activity. The period of 1944 through 1963 was in the heart of both the industrial revolution and the birth of the Baby Boom generation. Today, we are mired in extreme volatility with frequent periods of boom and bust at the same time we are witnessing the beginning of the greatest retirement wave ever experienced within the U.S. economy.

To contrast these two time periods in respect to the recovery period is almost asinine as the external pressures from globalization and domestic unfunded liabilities did not exist or were irrelevant factors during the prior period.

To add insult to injury, U.S. domestic unfunded liabilities are currently estimated somewhere around $61.6 trillion due to items such as Social Security, Medicare and government pensions. The most concerning part of this pertains to the coming wave of retirement as the Baby Boom generation begins retiring and drawing on the unfunded Social Security for which they currently have entitlement. Over the long run, expenditures related to healthcare programs such as Medicare and Medicaid are projected to grow faster than the economy overall as the population matures.

To put unfunded liabilities into perspective, consider these as off-balance-sheet obligations similar to those of Enron. Although these are not listed as part of the national debt, they must be paid. These liabilities exist outside of the annual budgetary debt discussed. The difference between Enron and the U.S. unfunded liabilities is that if the U.S. government cannot come up with the funds to pay all these liabilities through revenue generation, they will print the money necessary to pay the debt.

WHAT DOES THE SOLUTION LOOK LIKE?
Unfortunately, the general public is in a no-win situation for this solution to the problem. Printing money does not bode well for economic growth. This creates inflationary pressures that devalue the U.S. dollar and make everyone less wealthy. Cutting the entitlements that compose this liability leaves millions of people without benefits they have come to expect. The only other option, and one that the government knows all too well, is increasing taxes. In fact, according to a Congressional Budget Office paper issued in 2004:

"The term 'unfunded liability' has been used to refer to a gap between the government's projected financial commitment under a particular program and the revenues that are expected to be available to fund that commitment. But no government obligation can be truly considered 'unfunded' because of the U.S. government's sovereign power to tax—which is the ultimate resource to meet its obligations."

A balanced budget will be required at some point and with this will come higher taxes. We have uncertainty surrounding tax rates and how high they will go. At that time, extensions put in place in December 2010 on Bush-era tax cuts are set to expire. We are likely to see some tax increases at this point. Whether it is only on the top earners or unilaterally across all income levels is yet to be seen, but an increase of some sort will most certainly occur.

How do you prepare? Why spend so much time reassuring you that taxes will potentially increase? Because you have an opportunity to take action. Now is the time to prepare for what will come and structure countermeasures for the good, the bad and the ugly of each of these legislative nightmares through tax-advantaged retirement planning.

You usually make more money by saving on taxes than you do by making more money. The simplistic logic of the statement makes sense when you discover it takes $1.50 in earnings to put that same dollar, saved in taxes, back in your pocket.

As simple as it sounds, it is much more difficult to execute. Most people fail to put together a plan as they near retirement, beginning with a simple cash flow budget. If you have not analyzed your proposed income streams and expenses, you could not possibly have taken the time to position these cash flows and other events into a tax-preferred plan.

Most people will state that they have a plan and, thus, do not need any further assistance in this area. The truth in most instances is that people could not show you their plan, and among the few that could, most would not be able to show you how they have executed it. In this regard, they might as well be Richard Nixon stating, "I am not a crook" for as much as they state, "I have a plan." The truth lies in waiting. As we approach or begin retirement, we should look at what cash flows we will have. Do we have a pension? How about Social Security? How much additional cash flow am I going to need to draw from my assets to maintain the lifestyle that I desire?

We spend our whole lives saving and accumulating wealth but spend so little time determining how to distribute this accumulation so as to retain it. We need to make sure we have the appropriate diversification of taxable versus non-taxable assets to complement our distribution strategy.

THE BENEFITS OF DIVERSIFICATION

Heading into retirement, we should be situated with a diversified tax landscape. The point to spending our whole lives accumulating wealth is not to see the size of the number on paper, but rather to be an exercise in how much we put in our pocket after removing it from the paper. To truly understand tax diversification, we must understand what types of money exist and how each of these will be treated during accumulation and, most importantly, during distribution. The following is a brief summary:

1. Free money
2. Tax-advantaged money
3. Tax-deferred money
4. Taxable money
    a. Ordinary income
    b. Capital gains and qualified dividends

FREE MONEY

Free money is the best kind of money regardless of tax treatment because, in the end, you have more money than you would have otherwise. Many employers will provide contributions toward employee retirement accounts to offer additional employment benefits and encourage employees to save for their own retirement. With this, employers often will offer a matching contribution in which they contribute up to a certain percentage of an employee's salary (generally three to five percent) toward that employee's retirement account when the employee contributes to their retirement account as well. For example, if an employee earns $50,000 annually and contributes three percent ($1,500) to their retirement account annually, the employer will also contribute three percent ($1,500) to the employee's account. That is $1,500 in free money. Take all you can get! Bear in mind that any employer contribution to a 401(k) will still be subject to taxation when withdrawn.

TAX-ADVANTAGED MONEY

Tax-advantaged money is the next best thing to free money. Although you have to earn tax-advantaged money, you do not have to give part of it away to Uncle Sam. Tax-advantaged money comes in three basic forms that you can utilize during your lifetime; four if prison inspires your future, but we are not going to discuss that option.

One of the most commonly known forms of tax-advantaged money is municipal bonds, which earn and pay interest that could be tax-advantaged on the federal level, or state level, or both. There are several caveats that should be discussed with regard to the notion of tax-advantaged income from municipal bonds. First, you will notice that tax-advantaged has several flavors from the state and federal perspective. This is because states will generally tax the interest earned on a municipal bond unless the bond is offered from an entity located within that state. This severely limits the availability of completely tax-advantaged municipal bonds and constrains underlying risk and liquidity factors. Second, municipal bond interest is added back into the equation for determining your modified adjusted gross income (MAGI) for Social Security. This could push your income above a threshold and subject a portion of your Social Security income to taxation.

THE FUTURE OF U.S. TAXATION
In effect, if this interest subjects some other income to taxation then this interest is truly being taxed.

Last, municipal bond interest may be excluded from the regular federal tax system, but it is included for determining tax under the alternative minimum tax (AMT) system. In its basic form, the AMT system is a separate tax system that applies if the tax computed under AMT exceeds the tax computed under the regular tax system. The difference between these two computations is the alternative minimum tax.

TAX-ADVANTAGED MONEY: ROTH IRA
Roth accounts are probably the single greatest tax asset that has come from Congress outside of life insurance. They are well known but rarely used. Roth IRAs were first established by the Taxpayer Relief Act of 1997 and named after Senator William Roth, the chief sponsor of the legislation. Roth accounts are simply an account in the form of an individual retirement account or an employer sponsored retirement account that allows for tax-advantaged growth of earnings and, thus, tax-advantaged income.

The main difference between a Roth and a traditional IRA or employer-sponsored plan lies in the timing of the taxation. We are all very familiar with the typical scenario of putting money away for retirement through an employer plan, whereby they deduct money from our paychecks and put it directly into a retirement account. This money is taken out before taxes are calculated, meaning we do not pay tax on those earnings today. A Roth account, on the other hand, takes the money after the taxes have been removed and puts it into the retirement account, so we do pay tax on the money today. The other significant difference between these two is taxation during distribution in later years. Regarding our traditional retirement accounts, when we take the money out later it is added to our ordinary income and is taxed accordingly. Additionally, including this in our income subjects us to the consequences mentioned above for municipal bonds with Social Security taxation, AMT, as well as higher Medicare premiums. A Roth on the other hand is distributed tax-advantaged and does not contribute toward negative impact items such as Social Security taxation, AMT, or Medicare premium increases. It essentially comes back to us without tax and other obligations.

The best way to view the difference between the two accounts is to look at the life of a farmer. A farmer will buy seed, plant it in the ground, grow the crops and harvest it later for sale. Typically, the farmer would only pay tax on the crops that have been harvested and sold. But if you were the farmer, would you rather pay tax on the $5,000 of seed that you plant today or the $50,000 of crops harvested later? The obvious answer is $5,000 of seed today. The truth to the matter is that you are a farmer, except you plant dollars into your retirement account instead of seeds into the earth.

So why doesn't everyone have a Roth retirement account if things are so simple? There are several reasons, but the single greatest reason has been the constraints on contributions. If you earned over certain thresholds (MAGI over $125,000 single and $183,000 joint for 2012), you were not eligible to make contributions, and until last year, if your modified adjusted gross income (MAGI) was over $100,000 (single or joint), you could not convert a traditional IRA to a Roth. Outside these contribution limits, most people save for retirement through their employers and most employers do not offer Roth options in their plans. The reason behind this is because Roth accounts are not that well understood and people have been educated to believe that saving on taxes today is the best possible course of action.

TAX-ADVANTAGED MONEY: LIFE INSURANCE

As previously mentioned, the single greatest tax asset that has come from Congress outside of life insurance is the Roth account. Life insurance is the little-known or little-discussed tax asset that holds some of the greatest value in your financial history both during life and upon death. It is by far the best tax-advantaged device available. We traditionally view life insurance as a way to protect our loved ones from financial ruin upon our demise and it should be noted that everyone who cares about someone should have life insurance. Purchasing a life insurance policy ensures that our loved ones will receive income from the life insurance company to help them pay our final expenses and carry on with their lives without us comfortably when we die. The best part of the life insurance windfall is the fact that nobody will have to pay tax on the money received. This is the single greatest tax-advantaged device available, but it has one downside, we do not get to use it. Only our heirs will.

The little known and discussed part of life insurance is the cash value build-up within whole life and universal life (permanent) policies. Life insurance is not typically seen as an investment vehicle for building wealth and retirement planning, although we should discuss briefly why this thought process should be re-evaluated. Permanent life insurance is generally misconceived as something that is very expensive for a wealth accumulation vehicle because there are mortality charges (fees for the death benefit) that detract from the available returns. Furthermore, those returns do not yield as much as the stock market over the long run. This is why many times you will hear the phrase "buy term and invest the rest," where "term" refers to term insurance.

Let us take a second to review two terms just used in regard to life insurance: term and permanent. Term insurance is an idea with which most people are familiar. You purchase a certain death benefit that will go to your heirs upon death and this policy will be in effect for a certain number of years, typically 10 to 20 years. The 10 to 20 years is the term of the policy and once you have reached that end you no longer have insurance unless you purchase another policy.

Permanent insurance on the other hand has no term involved. It is permanent as long as the premiums continue to be paid. Permanent insurance generally initially has higher premiums than term insurance for the same amount of death benefit coverage and it is this difference that is referred to when people say "invest the rest."

Simply speaking there are significant differences between these two policies that are not often considered when providing a comparative analysis of the numbers. One item that gets lost in the fray when comparing term and permanent insurance is that term usually expires before death. In fact, insurance studies show less than one percent of all term policies pay out death benefit claims. The issue arises when the term expires and the desire to have more insurance is still present.

A term policy with the same benefit will be much more expensive than the original policy and, many times, life events occur, such as cancer or heart conditions, which makes it impossible to acquire another policy and leaves your loved ones unprotected and tax-advantaged legacy planning out of the equation.

Another aspect and probably the most important piece in consideration of the future of taxation is the fact that permanent insurance has a cash accumulation value. Two aspects stand out with the cash accumulation value. First, as the cash accumulation value increases the death benefit will also increase whereas term insurance remains level. Second, this cash accumulation offers value to you during your lifetime rather than to your heirs upon death. The cash accumulation value can be used for tax-advantaged income during your lifetime through policy loans. Most importantly, this tax-advantaged income is available during retirement for distribution planning, all while offering the same typical financial protection to your heirs.

TAX-DEFERRED MONEY

Tax-deferred money is the type of money with which most of people are familiar, but we also briefly reviewed the idea above. Tax-deferred money is typically our traditional IRA, employer sponsored retirement plan or a non-qualified annuity. Essentially, you put money into an investment vehicle that will accumulate in value over time and you do not pay taxes on the earnings that grow these accounts until you distribute them. Once the money is distributed, taxes must be paid. However, the same negative consequences exist with regard to additional taxation and expense in other areas as previously discussed. The cash accumulation value can be used for tax-advantaged income.

TAXABLE MONEY

Taxable money is everything else and is taxable today, later or whenever it is received. These four types of money come down to two distinct classifications: taxable and tax-free. The greatest difference when comparing taxable and tax-advantaged income is a function of how much money we keep after tax. For help in determining what the differences should be, excluding outside factors such as Social Security taxation and AMT, a tax equivalent yield should be used.

To put the tax equivalent yield into perspective, let us look at an example: Bob and Mary are currently retired, living on Social Security and interest from investments and falling within the 25 percent tax bracket. They have a substantial portion of their investments in municipal bonds yielding 6 percent, which is quite comforting in today's market. The tax equivalent yield they would need to earn from a taxable investment would be 8 percent, a 2 percent gap that seems almost impossible given current market volatility. However, something that has never been put into perspective is that the interest from their municipal bonds is subject to taxation on their Social Security benefits (at 21.25 percent). With this, the yield on their municipal bonds would be 4.725 percent, and the taxable equivalent yield falls to 6.3 percent, leaving a gap of only 1.575 percent.

In the end, most people spend their lives accumulating wealth through the best, if not the only vehicle they know, a tax-deferred account. This account is most likely a 401(k) or 403(b) plan offered through our employer and may be supplemented with an IRA that was established at one point or another. As the years go by, people blindly throw money into these accounts in an effort to save for a retirement that we someday hope to reach.

The truth is, most people have an age selected for when they would like to retire, but spend their lives wondering if they will ever be able to actually quit working. To answer this question, you must understand how much money you will have available to contribute toward your needs. *In other words, you need to know what your after-tax income will be during this period.*

All else being equal, it would not matter if you put your money into a taxable, tax-deferred or tax-advantaged account as long as income tax rates never change and outside factors are never an event. The net amount you receive in the end will be the same.

Unfortunately, this will never be the case. Many believe that taxes will increase in the future, meaning we will likely see higher taxes in retirement than during our peak earning years.

Regardless, saving for retirement in any form is a good thing as it appears from all practical perspectives that future government benefits will be cut and taxes will increase. You have the ability to plan today for efficient tax diversification and maximization of our after-tax dollars during your distribution years.

CHAPTER 12 RECAP //

- An effective retirement plan will take into account the tax implications of each of your investments. Having a tax-diversified portfolio can provide you with various strategies to use throughout retirement to help you save on your tax bill.
- Each investment has tax pros and cons. Traditional IRAs, for example, help you save on taxes during your working years, but they can create tax problems if taxes do go up during your retirement. Understand the tax pros and cons for every asset you own.
- Work with a team of professionals, including a financial and tax professional, to create and update your retirement plan so that it takes into account tax issues and changes.

13
THE ROTH IRA AND TAX PLANNING

"A good plan is like a road map: it shows the final destination and usually the best way to get there."
– H. Stanley Judd

Louis Brandeis provides one of the best examples illustrating how tax planning works. Brandeis was Associate Justice on the Supreme Court of the United States from 1916 to 1939. Born in Louisville, Kentucky, Brandeis was an intelligent man with a touch of country charm. He described tax planning this way:

"I live in Alexandria, Virginia. Near the Court Chambers, there is a toll bridge across the Potomac. When in a rush, I pay the dollar toll and get home early. However, I usually drive outside the downtown section of the city and cross the Potomac on a free bridge.

The bridge was placed outside the downtown Washington, D.C. area to serve a useful social service—getting drivers to drive the extra mile and help alleviate congestion during the rush hour.

If I went over the toll bridge and through the barrier without paying a toll, I would be committing tax evasion.

If I drive the extra mile and drive outside the city of Washington to the free bridge, I am using a legitimate, logical and suitable method of tax avoidance, and I am performing a useful social service by doing so.

*The tragedy is that **few people know that the free bridge exists**.*"

Like Brandeis, most American taxpayers have options when it comes to "crossing the Potomac," so to speak. It's a financial planner's job to tell you what options are available. You can wait until March to file your taxes, at which time you might pay someone to report and pay the government a larger portion of your income. However, you could instead file before the end of the year, work with your financial professional and incorporate a tax plan as part of your overall financial planning strategy. Filing later is like crossing the toll bridge. Tax planning is like crossing the free bridge.

Which would you rather do?

The answer to this question is easy. Most people want to save money and pay less in taxes. What makes this situation really difficult in real life, however, is that the signs along the side of the road that direct us to the free bridge are not that clear. To normal Americans, and to plenty of people who have studied it, the U.S. tax code is easy to get lost in. There are all kinds of rules, exceptions to rules, caveats and conditions that are difficult to understand, or even to know about. What you really need to know is your options and the bottom line impacts of those options.

ROTH IRA CONVERSIONS

The attractive qualities of Roth IRAs may have prompted you to explore the possibility of moving some of your assets into a Roth account. Another important difference between the accounts is how they treat Required Minimum Distributions (RMDs). When you turn 70 ½ years old, you are required to take a minimum amount of money out of a traditional IRA. This amount is your RMD. It is treated as taxable income. Roth IRAs, however, do not have RMDs, and their distributions are not taxable. Quite a deal, right?

While having a Roth IRA as part of your portfolio is a good idea, converting assets to a Roth IRA can pose some challenges, depending on what kinds of assets you want to transfer.

One common option is the conversion of a traditional IRA to a Roth IRA. You may have heard about converting your IRA to a Roth IRA, but you might not know the full net result on your income. The main difference between the two accounts is that the growth of investments within a traditional IRA is not taxed until income is withdrawn from the account, whereas taxes are charged on contribution amounts to a Roth IRA, not withdrawals. The problem, however, is that when assets are removed from a traditional IRA, even if the assets are being transferred to a Roth IRA account, taxes apply.

There are a lot of reasons to look at Roth conversions. People have a lot of money in IRAs, up to multiple millions of dollars. Even with $500,000, when they turn 70 ½ years old, their RMD is going to be approximately $18,000, and they have to take that out whether they want to or not. It's a tax issue. Essentially, if you will be subject to high RMDs, it could have impacts on how much of your Social Security is taxable, and on your tax bracket.

By paying taxes now instead of later on assets in a Roth IRA, you can realize tax-advantaged growth. You pay once and you're done paying. Your heirs are done paying. It's a powerful tool. Here's a simple example to show you how powerful it can be:

Imagine that you pay to convert a traditional IRA to a Roth. You have decided that you want to put the money in a vehicle that gives you a tax-advantaged income option down the road. If you pay a 25 percent tax on that conversion and the Roth IRA then doubles in value over the next 10 years, you could look at your situation as only having paid 12.5 percent tax.

The prospect of tax-advantaged income is a tempting one. While you have to pay a conversion tax to transfer your assets, you also have turned taxable income into tax-free retirement money that you can let grow as long as you want without being required to withdraw it.

There are options, however, that address this problem. Much like the Brandeis story, there may be a "free bridge" option for many investors.

Your financial professional will likely tell you that it is not a matter of whether or not you should perform a Roth IRA conversion, it is a matter of how much you should convert and when.

Here are some of the things to consider before converting to a Roth IRA:

- If you make a conversion before you retire, you may end up paying higher taxes on the conversion because it is likely that you are in some of your highest earning years, placing you in the highest tax bracket of your life. It is possible that a better strategy would be to wait until after you retire, a time when you may have less taxable income, which would place you in a lower tax bracket.
- Many people opt to reduce their work hours from full-time to part-time in the years before they retire. If you have pursued this option, your income will likely be lower, in turn lowering your tax rate.

- The first years that you draw Social Security benefits can also be years of lower reported income, making it another good time frame in which to convert to a Roth IRA.

One key strategy to handling a Roth IRA conversion is to *always be able to pay the cost of the tax conversion with outside money.* Structuring your tax year to include something like a significant deduction can help you offset the conversion tax. This way you aren't forced to take the money you need for taxes from the value of the IRA. The reason taxes apply to this maneuver is because when you withdraw money from a traditional IRA, the IRS treats it as taxable income. Your financial professional, with the help of the CPAs at their firm, may be able to provide you with options like after-tax money, itemized deductions or other situations that can pose effective tax avoidance options.

Some examples of avoiding Roth IRA conversions taxes include:
- *Using medical expenses that are above 10 percent of your Adjusted Gross Income.* If you have health care costs that you can list as itemized deductions, you can convert an amount of income from a traditional IRA to a Roth IRA that is offset by the deductible amount. Essentially, deductible medical expenses negate the taxes resulting from recording the conversion.
- *Individuals, usually small business owners, who are dealing with a Net Operating Loss (NOL).* If you have NOLs, but aren't able to utilize all of them on your tax return, you can carry them forward to offset the taxable income from the taxes on income you convert to a Roth IRA.
- *Charitable giving.* If you are charitably inclined, you can use the amount of your donations to reduce the amount of taxable income you have during that year. By matching the amount you convert to a Roth IRA to the amount

your taxable income was reduced by charitable giving, you can essentially avoid taxation on the conversion. You may decide to double your donations to a charity in one year, giving them two years' worth of donations in order to offset the Roth IRA conversion tax on this year's tax return.
- *Investments that are subject to depletion.* Certain investments can kick off depletion expenses. If you make an investment and are subject to depletion expenses, they can be deducted and used to offset a Roth IRA conversion tax.

Not all of the above scenarios work for everyone, and there are many other options for offsetting conversion taxes. The point is that you have options, and your financial professional and tax professional can help you understand those options.

If you have a traditional IRA, Roth conversions are something you should look at. As you approach retirement you should consider your options and make choices that keep more of your money in your pocket, not the government's.

ADDITIONAL TAX BENEFITS OF ROTH IRAS

Not only do Roth IRAs provide you with tax-advantaged growth, they also give you a tax-diversified landscape that allows you to maximize your distributions. Chances are that no matter the circumstances, you will have taxed income and other assets subject to taxation. *But if you have a Roth IRA, you have the unique ability to manage your Adjusted Gross Income (AGI), because you have a tax-advantaged income option!*

Converting to a Roth IRA can also help you preserve and build your legacy. Because Roth IRAs are exempt from RMDs, after you make a conversion from a traditional IRA, your Roth account can grow tax-advantaged for another 15, 20 or 25 years and it can be used as tax-advantaged income by your heirs. It is important to note, however, that non-spousal beneficiaries do have to take RMDs from a Roth IRA, or choose to stretch it and draw tax-advantaged income out of it over their lifetime.

TO CONVERT OR NOT TO CONVERT?
Conversions aren't only for retirees. You can convert at any time. Your choice should be based on your individual circumstances and tax situation. Sticking with a traditional IRA or converting to a Roth, again, depends on your individual circumstances, including your income, your tax bracket and the amount of deductions you have each year.

Is it better to have a Roth IRA or traditional IRA? It depends on your individual circumstance. Some people don't mind having taxable income from an IRA. Their income might not be very high and their RMD might not bump their tax bracket up, so it's not as big a deal. A similar situation might involve income from Social Security. Social Security benefits are taxed based on other income you are drawing. If you are in a position where none or very little of your Social Security benefit is subject to taxes, paying income tax on your RMD may be very easy.

> *There are also situations where leveraging taxable income from a traditional IRA can work to your advantage come tax time. For example, Darrel and Linda dream of buying a boat when they retire. It is something they have looked forward to their entire marriage. In addition to the savings and investments that they created to supply them with income during retirement, which include a traditional IRA, they have also saved money for the sole purpose of purchasing a boat once they stop working.*
>
> *When the time comes and they finally buy the boat of their dreams, they pay an additional $15,000 in sales taxes that year because of the large purchase. Because they are retired*

and earning less money, the deductions they used to be able to realize from their income taxes are no longer there. The high amount of sales taxes they paid on the boat puts them in a position where they could benefit from taking taxable income from a traditional IRA.

When Darrel and Linda's financial professional learns about their purchase, he immediately contacts a CPA at his firm to run the numbers. They determine that by taking a $15,000 distribution from their IRA, they could fulfill their income needs to offset the $15,000 sales tax deduction that they were claiming due to the purchase of their boat. In the end, they pay zero taxes on their income distribution from their IRA.

The moral of the story? **Having a tax-diversified landscape gives you options.** Having capital assets that can be liquidated, tax-advantaged income options and sources that can create capital gains or capital losses will put you in a position to play your cards right no matter what you want to accomplish with your taxes. The ace up your sleeve is your financial professional and the CPAs they work with. Do yourself a favor and *plan* your taxes instead of *reporting* them!

CHAPTER 13 RECAP //

- Look for the "free bridge" option in your tax strategy.
- Converting from a traditional to a Roth IRA can provide you with tax-advantaged retirement income.
- Converting to a Roth IRA can also help you preserve and build your legacy.
- There are many ways to reduce your taxes. Being smart about your Roth IRA conversion is one of the main ways to do so.

14
WHAT KIND OF LEGACY WILL YOU LEAVE?

"Carve your name on hearts, not tombstones. A legacy is etched into the minds of others and the stories they share about you."
— Shannon L. Alder

Betty and I worked together for many . At the end of every meeting, before we said goodbye, she would say, "Tell me your promise." My job, which she explained to me on the day we met for the first time, was to reply, "I promise I will take care of your kids when you pass away."

I said it, and I meant it. One day, I received the phone call that I knew would come soon. Betty's daughter Mable called to tell me that overnight, comfortable and in her own bed, Betty had died. I asked

Mable when I might get on the phone with all of the siblings to go over everything, and we settled on a time. The next day, I sat in the conference room where I had held my calls with Betty so many times, except this time I was starting the process of fulfilling my promise.

I helped Betty's kids work with the Social Security Administration to stop their mother's payments, and I took care of settling all of her accounts and distributed all of the assets in the estate, exactly like Betty had asked me to. I walked them through every step of the process, and I tried to take as much off of their shoulders as I could.

Over several appointments and during numerous hours on the phone with all of them, each of Betty's kids thanked me for the time I was spending. A few of them confessed that they had worried about me acting as their mother's advisor, especially since I moved to a different state in the middle of our working relationship. "Mom has always told us, 'Just call Tim if you need anything,' and now we know that was true." Today, I'm the advisor for all of Betty's kids.

If you're like most people, planning your estate isn't on the top of your list of things to do. Planning your income needs for retirement, managing your assets and just living your life without worrying about how your estate will be handled when you are gone make legacy planning less than attractive for a Saturday afternoon task. The fact of the matter, however, is that if you don't plan your legacy, someone else will. That someone else is usually a combination of the IRS and other government entities: lawyers, executors, courts, and accountants. Who do you think has the best interests of your beneficiaries in mind?

Today, there is more consideration given to planning a legacy than just maximizing your estate. When most people think about an estate, it may seem like something only the very wealthy have: a stately manor or an enormous business. But a legacy is something else entirely. A legacy is more than the sum total of the financial assets you have accumulated. It is the lasting impressions you make on those you leave behind. The dollar and cents are just a small part of a legacy.

A legacy encompasses the stories that others tell about you, shared experiences and values. An estate may pay for college tuition, but a legacy may inform your grandchildren about the importance of higher education and self-reliance.

A legacy may also contain family heirlooms or items of emotional significance. It may be a piece of art your great-grandmother painted, family photos, or a childhood keepsake.

When you go about planning your legacy, certainly explore strategies that can maximize the financial benefit to the ones you care about. But also take the time to ensure that you have organized the whole of your legacy, and let that be a part of the last gift you leave.

Many people avoid planning their legacy until they feel they must. Something may change in your life, like the birth of a grandchild, the diagnosis of a serious health problem, or the death of a close friend or loved one. Waiting for tragedy to strike in order to get your affairs in order is not the best course of action. The emotional stress of that kind of situation can make it hard to make patient, thoughtful decisions. Taking the time to create a premeditated and thoughtful legacy plan will assure that your assets will be transferred where and when you want them when the time comes.

THE BENEFITS OF PLANNING YOUR LEGACY

The distribution of your assets, whether in the form of property, stocks, Individual Retirement Accounts, 401(k)s or liquid assets, can be a complicated undertaking if you haven't left clear instructions about how you want them handled. Not having a plan will cost more money and take more time, leaving your loved ones to wait (sometimes for years) and receive less of your legacy than if you had a clear plan.

Planning your legacy will help your assets be transferred with little delay and little confusion. Instead of leaving decisions about how to distribute your estate to your family, attorneys or financial professionals, preserve your legacy and your wishes by drafting a clear plan at an early age.

And while you know all that, it can still be hard to sit down and do it. It reminds you that life is short, and the relatively complicated nature of sorting through your assets can feel like a daunting task. But one thing is for sure: ***it is impossible for your assets to be transferred or distributed the way you want at the end of your life if you don't have a plan.***

Ask yourself:
- Are my assets up to date?
- Have my primary and contingent beneficiaries been clearly designated?
- Does my plan allow for restriction of a beneficiary?
- Does my legacy plan address minor children that I want to provide with income?
- Does my legacy plan allow for multi-generational payout?

Answers to these questions are critical if you want the final say in how your assets are distributed. In order to achieve your legacy goals, you need a plan.

MAKING A PLAN

Eventually, when your income need is filled and you have sufficient standby money to meet your need for emergencies, travel or other extra expenses you are planning for, whatever isn't used during your lifetime becomes your financial legacy. The money that you do not use during your lifetime will either go to loved ones, unloved ones, charity, or the IRS. The question is, who would you rather disinherit?

By having a legacy plan that clearly outlines your assets, your beneficiaries and your distribution goals, you can make sure that your money and property is ending up in the hands of the people you determine beforehand. Is it really that big of a deal? It absolutely is. Think about it. Without a clear plan, it is impossible for anyone to know if your beneficiary designations are current and reflect your wishes because you haven't clearly expressed who your beneficiaries are. You may have an idea of who you want your assets to go to, but without a plan, it is anyone's guess. It is also impossible to know if the titling of your assets is accurate unless you have gone through and determined whose name is on the titles. More importantly, *if you have not clearly and effectively communicated your desires regarding the planned distribution of your legacy, you and your family may end up losing a large part of it.*

As you can see, managing a legacy is more complicated than having an attorney read your will, divide your estate and write checks to your heirs. The additional issue of taxes, Family Maximum Benefit calculations and a host of other decisions rear their heads. Educating yourself about the best options for positioning your legacy assets is a challenging undertaking. Working with a financial professional who is versed in determining the most efficient and effective ways of preserving and distributing your legacy can save you time, money and strife.

So, how do you begin?

Making a Legacy Plan Starts with a Simple List. The first, and one of the largest, steps to setting up an estate plan with a financial professional that reflects your desires is creating a detailed inventory of your assets and debts (if you have any). You need to know what assets you have, who the beneficiaries are, how much they are worth and how they are titled. You can start by identifying and listing your assets. This is a good starting point for working with a financial professional who can then help you determine the detailed information about your assets that will dictate how they are distributed upon your death.

If you are particularly concerned about leaving your kids and grandkids a lifetime of income with minimal taxes, you will want to discuss a Stretch IRA option with your financial professional.

STRETCH IRAS: GETTING THE MOST OUT OF YOUR MONEY

In 1986, the U.S. Congress passed a law that allows for multi-generational distributions of IRA assets. This type of distribution is called a Stretch IRA because it stretches the distribution of the account out over a longer period of time to several beneficiaries. It also allows the account to continue accumulating value throughout your relatives' lifetimes. You can use a Stretch IRA as an income tool that distributes throughout your lifetime, your children's lifetimes and your grandchildren's lifetimes.

Stretch IRAs are an attractive option for those more concerned with creating income for their loved ones than leaving them with a lump sum that may be subject to a high tax rate. With traditional IRA distributions, non-spousal beneficiaries must generally take distributions from their inherited IRAs, whether transferred or not, within five years after the death of the IRA owner. An exception to this rule applies if the beneficiary elects to take distributions over his or her lifetime, which is referred to as stretching the IRA.

Let's begin by looking at the potential of stretching an IRA throughout multiple generations.

> » *In this scenario, Mr. Cleaver has an IRA with a current balance of $350,000. If we assume a five percent annual rate of return, and a 28 percent tax rate, the Stretch IRA turned a $502,625 legacy into more than $1.5 million. Doubling*

the value of the IRA also provided Mr. Cleaver, his wife, two children and three grandchildren with income. Not choosing the stretch option would have cost nearly $800,000 and had impacts on six of Mr. Cleaver's loved ones.

Unfortunately, many things may also play a role in failing to stretch IRA distributions. It can be tempting for a beneficiary to

Beneficiaries Stretch IRA Distributions

- Mr. Cleaver's IRA Value at 64: $350,000
- Mr. Cleaver's income from age 70-85: $383,251
- Mr. Cleaver passes away at 85
- Mrs. Cleaver passes away at 88
- Mrs. Cleaver's income from age 83-88: $180,048
- Mrs. Cleaver's IRA Value: $453,165

Wally receives income of:	Beaver receives income of:	Eddie receives income of:	Lumpy receives income of:	Gilbert receives income of:
$133,971*	$144,008*	$293,717*	$313,799*	$345,752*

TOTAL INCOME TO ALL - IRA STRETCH CONCEPT: $1,231,248
Scenario assumes a 28 percent tax rate with annual rate of return of 5 percent
*Income based on RMDs of beneficiaries

Beneficiaries FAIL to Stretch IRA Distributions

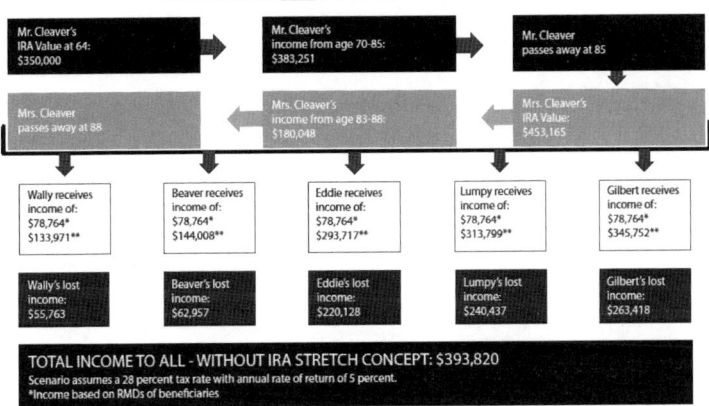

- Mr. Cleaver's IRA Value at 64: $350,000
- Mr. Cleaver's income from age 70-85: $383,251
- Mr. Cleaver passes away at 85
- Mrs. Cleaver passes away at 88
- Mrs. Cleaver's income from age 83-88: $180,048
- Mrs. Cleaver's IRA Value: $453,165

Wally receives income of:	Beaver receives income of:	Eddie receives income of:	Lumpy receives income of:	Gilbert receives income of:
$78,764*	$78,764*	$78,764*	$78,764*	$78,764*
$133,971**	$144,008**	$293,717**	$313,799**	$345,752**

Wally's lost income:	Beaver's lost income:	Eddie's lost income:	Lumpy's lost income:	Gilbert's lost income:
$55,763	$62,957	$220,128	$240,437	$263,418

TOTAL INCOME TO ALL - WITHOUT IRA STRETCH CONCEPT: $393,820
Scenario assumes a 28 percent tax rate with annual rate of return of 5 percent.
*Income based on RMDs of beneficiaries

* Lump sum after tax income upon death of Mrs. Cleaver.   ** Lifetime income based on RMD of beneficiary - see above.

take a lump sum of money despite the tax consequences. Fortunately, if you want to solidify your plan for distribution, there are options that will allow you to open up an IRA and incorporate "spendthrift" clauses for your beneficiaries. This will ensure your legacy is stretched appropriately and to your specifications. Only certain insurance companies allow this option, and you will not find this benefit with any brokerage accounts. You need to work with a financial professional who has the appropriate relationship with an insurance company that provides this option.

CHAPTER 14 RECAP //

- Like tax planning, legacy planning is for everyone, not just the super wealthy. An investment advisor can help you identify strategies that will allow you to leave a lasting legacy even if you don't have huge sums of extra money.
- Effective legacy plans take into account taxes, Family Maximum Benefit calculations and a host of other concerns. By choosing to plan your legacy with a financial professional, you can save time, money and stress for both yourself and your heirs.
- Consider a stretch IRA, which can offer one option for extending your legacy, and reducing the tax liability owed by your heirs.

15
PLANNING A SUCCESSFUL LEGACY

"The only thing you take with you when you're gone is what you leave behind."
– John Allston

David organized his assets long ago. He started planning his retirement early and made investment decisions that would meet his needs. With a combination of IRA to Roth IRA conversions, a series of income annuities and a well-planned money management strategy overseen by his financial professional, he easily filled his income gap and was able to focus on ways to accumulate his wealth throughout his retirement. He reorganized his Know So and Hope So Money as he got older. When David retired, he had an income plan created that allowed him to maximize his Social Security benefit. He even had enough to accumulate wealth during his retirement. At this point, David turned *his attention to planning his legacy. He wanted to know how he could maximize the amount of his legacy he will pass on to his heirs.*

David met with an attorney to draw up a will, but he quickly learned that while having a will was a good plan, it wasn't the most efficient way to distribute his legacy. In fact, relying solely on a will created several roadblocks.

The two main problems that arose for David were *Probate* and *Unintentional Disinheritance:*

Problem #1: Probate
Probate. Just speaking the word out loud can cause shivers to run down your spine. Probate's ugly reputation is well deserved. It can be a costly, time consuming process that diminishes your estate and can delay the distribution of your estate to your loved ones. Nasty stuff, by any measure. Unless you have made a clear legacy plan and discussed options for avoiding probate, it is highly likely that you have many assets that might pass through probate needlessly. ***If your will and beneficiary designations aren't correctly structured, some of these assets will go through the probate process, which can turn dollars into cents.***

If you have a will, probate is usually just a formality. There is little risk that your will won't be executed per your instructions. The problem arises when the costs and lengthy timeline that probate creates come into play. Probate proceedings are notoriously expensive, lengthy and ponderous. A typical probate process identifies all of your assets and debts, pays any taxes and fees that you owe (including estate tax), pays court fees, and distributes your property and assets to your heirs. This process usually takes at least a year, and can take even longer before your heirs actually receive anything that you have left for them. For this reason, and because of the sometimes-exorbitant fees that may be charged by lawyers and accountants during the process, probate has earned a nasty reputation.

Probate can also be a painstakingly public process. Because the probate process happens in court, the assets you own that go through a probate procedure become part of the public record. While this may not seem like a big deal to some, other people don't want that kind of intimate information available to the public.

Additionally, if your estate is entirely distributed via your will, the money that your family may need to cover the costs of your medical bills, funeral expenses and estate taxes will be tied up in probate, which can last up to a year or more. While immediate family members may have the option of requesting immediate cash from your assets during probate to cover immediate health care expenses, taxes, and fees, that process comes with its own set of complications. Choosing alternative methods for distributing your legacy can make life easier for your loved ones and can help them claim more of your estate in a more timely fashion than traditional methods.

A simpler and less tedious approach is to avoid probate altogether by structuring your estate to be distributed outside of the probate process. Two common ways of doing this are by structuring your assets inside a life insurance plan, and by using individual retirement planning tools like IRAs that give you the option of designating a beneficiary upon your death.

Problem #2: Unintentionally Disinheriting Your Family
You would never want to unintentionally disinherit a loved one or loved ones because of confusion surrounding your legacy plan. Unfortunately, it happens. Why? This terrible situation is typically caused by a simple lack of understanding. In particular, mistakes regarding legacy distribution occur with regards to those whom people care for the most: their grandchildren.

One of the most important ways to plan for the inheritance of your grandchildren is by properly structuring the distribution of

your legacy. Specifically, you need to know if your legacy is going to be distributed *per stirpes* or *per capita*.
- **Per Stirpes.** *Per stirpes* is a legal term in Latin that means "by the branch." Your estate will be distributed *per stirpes* if you designate each branch of your family to receive an equal share of your estate. In the event that your children predecease you, their share will be distributed evenly between their children—your grandchildren.
- **Per Capita.** *Per capita* distribution is different in that you may designate different amounts of your estate to be distributed to members of the same generation.

Per stirpes distribution of assets will follow the family tree down the line as the predecessor beneficiaries pass away. On the other hand, per capita distribution of assets ends on the branch of the family tree with the death of a designated beneficiary. For example, when your child passes away, in a per capita distribution, your grandchildren would not receive distributions from the assets that you designated to your child.

What the terms mean is not nearly as important as what they do, however. The reality is that improperly titled assets could accidentally leave your grandchildren disinherited upon the death of their parents. It's easy to check, and it's even easier to fix.

A simple way to remember the difference between the two types of distribution goes something like this: "***Stirpes are forever and Capita is capped.***"

Another way to avoid complicated legacy distribution problems, and the probate process, is by leveraging a life insurance plan.

LIFE INSURANCE: AN IMPORTANT LEGACY TOOL

One of the most powerful legacy tools you can leverage is a good life insurance policy. Life insurance is a highly efficient legacy tool because it creates money when it is needed or desired the most. Over the years, life insurance has become less expensive, while it offers more features, and it provides longer guarantees.

There are many unique benefits of life insurance that can help your beneficiaries get the most out of your legacy. Some of them include:
- Providing beneficiaries with a tax-free, liquid asset.
- Covering the costs associated with your death.
- Providing income for your dependents.
- Offering an investment opportunity for your beneficiaries.
- Covering expenses such as tuition or mortgage down payments for your children or grandchildren.

Very few people want life insurance, but nearly everyone wants what it does. Life insurance is specifically, and uniquely, capable of creating money when it is needed most. When a loved one passes, no amount of money can remove the pain of loss. And certainly, money doesn't solve the challenges that might arise with losing someone important.

It has been said that when you have money, you have options. When you don't have money, your options are severely limited. You might imagine a life insurance policy can give your family and loved ones options that would otherwise be impossible.

> » Ben spent the last 20 years building a small business. In so many ways, it is a family business. Each of his three children, Maddie, Ruby and Edward, worked in the shop part-time during high school. But after all three attended college, only Maddie returned to join her father, and eventually will run the business full-time when Ben retires.
>
> Ben is able to retire comfortably on Social Security and on-going income from the shop, but the business is nearly his entire financial legacy. It is his wish that Maddie own the

business outright, but he also wants to leave an equal legacy to each of his three children.

There is no simple way to divide the business into thirds and still leave the business intact for Maddie.

Ben ends up buying a life insurance policy to make up the difference. Ruby and Edward will receive their share of an inheritance in cash from the life insurance policy and Maddie will be able to inherit the business intact.

Ben is able to accomplish his goals, treat all three children equitably and leave Maddie the business she helped to build.

If you have a life insurance policy but you haven't looked at it in a while, you may not know how it operates, how much it is worth and how it will be distributed to your beneficiaries. You may also need to update your beneficiaries on your policy. In short, without a comprehensive review of your policy, you don't really know where the money will go or to whom it will go.

If you don't have a life insurance policy but are looking for options to maintain and grow your legacy, speaking with a professional can show you the benefits of life insurance. Many people don't consider buying a life insurance policy until some event in their life triggers it, like the loss of a loved one, an accident or a health condition.

BENEFITS OF LIFE INSURANCE

Life insurance is a useful and secure tool for contingency planning, ensuring that your dependents receive the assets that you want them to have, and for meeting the financial goals you have set for the future. While it bears the name "Life Insurance," it is, in reality, a diverse financial tool that can meet many needs. The main function of a life insurance policy is to provide financial assets for your survivors. Life insurance is particularly efficient at achieving this goal because it provides a tax-advantaged lump sum of money in the form of a death benefit to your beneficiary or beneficiaries. That financial asset can be used in a number of ways. It can be structured as an investment to provide income for your spouse or children, it can pay down debts, and it can be used to cover estate taxes and other costs associated with death.

Tax liabilities on the estate you leave behind are inevitable. Capital property, for instance, is taxed at its fair market value at the time of your death, unless that property is transferred to your spouse. If the property has appreciated during the time you owned it, taxation on capital gains will occur. Registered Retirement Savings Plans (RRSPs) and other similarly structured assets are also included as taxable income unless transferred to a beneficiary as well. Those are just a few examples of how an estate can become subject to a heavy tax burden. The unique benefits of a life insurance policy provide ways to handle this tax burden, solving any liquidity problems that may arise if your family members want to hold onto an illiquid asset, such as a piece of property or an investment. Life insurance can provide a significant amount of money to a family member or other beneficiary, and that money is likely to remain exempt from taxation or seizure.

One of life insurance's most important benefits is that it is not considered part of the estate of the policyholder. The death benefit that is paid by the insurance company goes exclusively to the beneficiaries listed on the policy. This shields the proceeds of the policy from fees and costs that can reduce an estate, including probate proceedings, attorneys' fees and claims made by creditors. The distribution of your life insurance policy is also unaffected by delays of the estate's distribution, like probate. Your beneficiaries will get the proceeds of the policy in a timely fashion, regardless of how long it takes for the rest of your estate to be settled.

Investing a portion of your assets in a life insurance policy can also protect that portion of your estate from creditors. If you owe money to someone or some entity at the time of your death, a creditor is not able to claim any money from a life insurance policy or a fixed or variable annuity, for that matter. An exception to this rule is if you had already used the life insurance policy as collateral against a loan. If a large portion of the money you want to dedicate to your legacy is sitting in a savings account, investment or other liquid form, creditors may be able to receive their claim on it before your beneficiaries get anything, that is if there's anything left. A life insurance policy protects your assets from creditors and ensures that your beneficiaries get the money that you intend them to have.

HOW MUCH LIFE INSURANCE DO YOU NEED?

Determining the type of policy and the amount right for you depends on an analysis of your needs. A financial professional can help you complete a needs analysis that will highlight the amount of insurance that you require to meet your goals. This type of personalized review will allow you to determine ways to continue providing income for your spouse or any dependents you may have. A financial professional can also help you calculate the amount of income that your policy should replace to meet the needs of your beneficiaries and the duration of the distribution of that income.

You may also want to use your life insurance policy to meet any expenses associated with your death. These can include funeral costs, fees from probate and legal proceedings, and taxes. You may also want to dedicate a portion of your policy proceeds to help fund tuition or other expenses for your children or grandchildren. You can buy a policy and hope it covers all of those costs, or you can work with a professional who can calculate exactly how much insurance you need and how to structure it to meet your goals. Which would you rather do?

AVOIDING POTENTIAL SNAGS

There are benefits to having life insurance supersede the direction given in a will or other estate plan, but there are also some potential snags that you should address to meet your wishes. For example, if your will instructs that your assets be divided equally between your two children but your life insurance beneficiary is listed as just one of the children, the assets in the life insurance policy will only be distributed to the child listed as the beneficiary. The beneficiary designation of your life insurance supersedes your will's instruction. This is important to understand when designating beneficiaries on a policy you purchase. Work with a professional to make sure that your beneficiaries are accurately listed on your assets, especially your life insurance policies.

USING LIFE INSURANCE TO BUILD YOUR LEGACY

Depending on your goals, there are strategies you can use that could multiply how much you leave behind. Life insurance is one of the most surefire and efficient investment tools for building a substantial legacy that will meet your financial goals.

Here is a brief overview of how life insurance can boost your legacy:
- Life insurance provides an immediate increase in your legacy.
- It provides an income tax-advantaged death benefit for your beneficiaries.
- A good life insurance policy has the opportunity to accumulate value over time.
- It may have an option to include long-term care (LTC) or chronic illness benefits should you require them.

If your Green Money income needs for retirement are met and you have Yellow Money assets that will provide for your future expenses, you may have extra assets that you want to earmark as legacy funds. By electing to invest those assets into a life insurance policy, you can immediately increase the amount of your legacy. Remember, **life insurance allows you to transfer a tax-advantaged lump sum of money to your beneficiaries. It remains in your control during your lifetime, can provide for your long-term care needs and bypasses probate costs.** And make no mistake, taxes can have a huge impact on your legacy. Not only that, income and assets from your legacy can have tax implications for your beneficiaries, as well.

Here's a brief overview of how taxes could affect your legacy and your beneficiaries:

- The higher your income, the higher the rate at which it is taxed.
- Withdrawals from qualified plans are taxed as income.
- What's more, when you leave a large qualified plan, it ends up being taxed at a high rate.
- If you left a $500,000 IRA to your child, they could end up owing as much as $140,000 in income taxes.
- However, if you could just withdraw $50,000 a year, the tax bill might only be $10,000 per year.

How could you use that annual amount to leave a larger legacy? Luckily, you can leverage a life insurance policy to avoid those tax penalties, preserving a larger amount of your legacy and freeing your beneficiaries from an added tax burden.

> *» When Brenda turned 70 years old, she decided it was time to look into life insurance policy options. She still feels young, but she remembers that her mother died in early 70s, and she wants to plan ahead so she can pass on some of her legacy to her grandchildren just like her grandmother did for her.*
>
> *Brenda doesn't really want to think about life insurance, but she does want the security, reliability and tax-advantaged*

distribution that it offers. She lives modestly, and her Social Security benefit meets most of her income needs. As the beneficiary of her late husband's Certificate of Deposit (CD), she has $100,000 in an account that she has never used and doesn't anticipate ever needing since her income needs were already met.

After looking at several different investment options with a professional, Brenda decides that a Single Premium life insurance policy fits her needs best. She can buy the policy with a $100,000 one-time payment and she is guaranteed that it would provide more than the value of the contract to her beneficiaries. If she left the money in the CD, it would be subject to taxes. But for every dollar that she puts into the life insurance policy, her beneficiaries are guaranteed at least that dollar plus a death benefit, and all of it will be **tax-free!**

For $100,000, Brenda's particular policy offers a $170,000 death benefit distribution to her beneficiaries. By moving the $100,000 from a CD to a life insurance policy, Brenda increases her legacy by 70 percent. Not only that, she has also sheltered it from taxes, so her beneficiaries will be able to receive $1.70 for every $1.00 that she entered into the policy! While buying the policy doesn't allow her to use the money for herself, it does allow her family to benefit from her well-planned legacy.

MAKE YOUR WISHES KNOWN

Estate taxes used to be a much hotter topic in the mid-2000s when the estate tax limits and exclusions were much smaller and taxed at a higher rate than today. In 2008, estates valued at $2 million or more were taxed at 45 percent. Just two years later, the limit was raised to $5 million dollars taxed at 35 percent. The limit has continued to rise ever since. The limit applies to fewer people than before. Estate organization, however, is just as important as ever, and it affects everyone.

Ask yourself:
- Are your assets actually titled and held the way you think they are?
- Are your beneficiaries set up the way you think they should be?
- Have there been changes to your family or those you desire as beneficiaries?

There is more to your legacy beyond your property, money, investments and other assets that you leave to family members, loved ones and charities. Everyone has a legacy beyond money. You also leave behind personal items of importance, your values and beliefs, your personal and family history, and your wishes. Beyond a will and a plan for your assets, it is important that you make your wishes known to someone for the rest of your personal legacy. When it comes time for your family and loved ones to make decisions after you are gone, knowing your wishes can help them make decisions that honor you and your legacy, and give meaning to what you leave behind. Your professional can help you organize.

Think about your:
- Personal stories / recollections
- Values
- Personal items of emotional significance
- Financial assets

Do you want to make a plan to pass these things on to your family?

WORKING WITH A PROFESSIONAL

Part of using life insurance to your greatest advantage is selecting the policy and provider that can best meet your goals. Venturing into the jungle of policies, brokers and salespeople can be overwhelming, and can leave you wondering if you've made the best decision. Working with a trusted financial professional can help you cut through the red tape, the "sales-speak" and confusion to find a policy that meets your goals and best serves your desires for your money. If you already have a policy, a financial professional can help you review it and become familiar with the policy's premium, the guarantees the policy affords, its performance, and its features and benefits. A financial professional can also help you make any necessary changes to the policy.

> *When Cheryl turned 88, her daughter finally convinced her to meet with a financial professional to help her organize her assets and get her legacy in order. Although Cheryl is reluctant to let a stranger in on her personal finances, she ends up very glad that she did.*
>
> *In the process of listing Cheryl's assets and her beneficiaries, her professional finds a man's name listed as the beneficiary of an old life insurance annuity that she owns. It turns out, the man is Cheryl's ex-husband who is still alive. Had Cheryl passed away before her ex-husband, the annuities and any death benefits that came with them, would have been passed on to her ex-husband. This does not reflect her latest wishes.*

Things change, relationships evolve and the way you would like your legacy organized needs to adapt to the changes that happen throughout your life. There may be a new child or grandchild in your family, or you may have been divorced or remarried. A professional will regularly review your legacy assets and ask you questions to make sure that everything is up to date and that the current organization reflects your current wishes.

CHAPTER 15 RECAP //

- You can structure your assets in ways that maximize distributions to your beneficiaries.
- Working with a financial professional can help ensure that many of your assets avoid the ponderous and expensive probate process.
- A financial professional can help review the details of the assets you have designated to be a part of your legacy and make sure that you aren't unintentionally disinheriting your heirs.
- Life insurance provides the distribution of tax-free, liquid assets to your beneficiaries.
- Investing in a life insurance policy can significantly build your legacy
- Organizing your estate will allow you to make sure your wishes are properly carried through.
- You can take advantage of a "Stretch IRA" to provide income for you, your spouse and your beneficiaries throughout their lifetimes.
- Understand if your assets will be distributed *per stirpes* or *per capita*.
- Working with a financial professional can help you select the policy that best meets your needs, or can help you fine tune your existing policy to better reflect your desires and intentions.

16
FINDING THE RIGHT INVESTMENT ADVISOR

"Many brokers call themselves 'financial consultants,' or 'financial advisors.' But they are not the same as independent investment advisors."
– Warren Buffett

From the moment you dip your toes into the retirement planning pool to the point you start swimming laps, your assets organized, your income needs met, and your accumulation and legacy plans in place, working with a professional that you trust can make all the difference in how well your retirement reflects your desires.

It is important to know what you are looking for before taking the plunge. There are many people that would love to handle your money, but not everyone is qualified to handle it in a way that leads to a holistic approach to creating a solid retirement plan.

The distinction being made here is that you should look for someone that puts your interests first and actively wants to help you meet your goals and objectives. Oftentimes, the solutions someone sells you matter less than their dedication to making sure that you have a plan that meets your needs.

Professionals take your whole financial position into consideration. They make plans that adjust your risk exposure, invest in tools that secure your desired income during retirement and create investment strategies that allow you to continue accumulating wealth during your retirement for you to use later or to contribute to your legacy. If you buy stocks with a broker, use a different agent for a life insurance policy and have an unmanaged 401(k) through your employer, working with a financial professional will consolidate the management of your assets so you have one trustworthy person quarterbacking all of the team elements of your portfolio. Financial solutions and investment tools change, but the concepts that lie behind wise retirement planning are lasting. In the end, a financial professional's approach is designed for those serious about planning for retirement. *Can you say the same thing about the person that advises you about your financial life?*

It's easy to see how choosing a financial professional can be one of the most important decisions you can make in your life. Not only do they provide you with advice, they also manage the personal assets that supply your retirement income and contribute to your legacy. So, how do you find a good one?

HOW TO FIND A FINANCIAL PROFESSIONAL YOU CAN TRUST

Taking care to select a financial professional is one of the best things you can do for yourself and for your future. Your professional has influence and control of your investment decisions, making their role in your life more than just important. Your financial security and the quality of your retirement depend on the decisions, investment strategies and asset structuring that you and your professional create.

Working with a professional is different than calling up a broker when you want to buy or trade some stock. This isn't a decision that you can hand off to anyone else. You need to bring your time and attention to the table when it comes to finding someone with whom you can entrust your financial life. Separating the wheat from the chaff will take some work, but you'll be happy you did it.

While no one can tell you exactly who to choose or how to choose them, the following information can help you narrow the field:

- You can start by asking your friends, family and colleagues for referrals. You will want to pay particular attention to the recommendations that you get from others who are in your similar financial situation and who have similar lifestyle choices. The professional for the CEO of your company may have a different skill-set than the skill-set of the professional befitting your cousin who has three kids and a Subaru like you. Do follow-up research on the internet as well. Look up the people who have been recommended to you on websites like LinkedIn that show the work history, referrals and experience of the candidates that you find most attractive. You will also learn about the firms with or for whom they work. The investment philosophies and reputations of the companies they work for will tell you a lot about how they will handle your money.
- The other side of the coin, however, is that everyone and their brother has a recommendation about how you should manage your money and who should manage it for you. From hot stock tips to "the best money manager in the state," people love to share good information that makes them look like they are in the know. Nobody wants to talk

about the bad stock purchases they made, the times they lost money and the poor selections they made regarding financial professionals or stock brokers. If you decide to take a friend or family member's recommendation, make sure they have a substantial, long-term experience with the financial professional and that their glowing review isn't just based on a one-time "win."
- It is important to understand how your professional is being paid. It is generally considered preferable to work with a fee-based professional who will not have conflicts of interests between earning a commission and acting in your best interests.
- Many professionals may also be brokers or dealers that can earn commissions on things like life insurance, certain types of annuities and disability insurance. These professionals have most likely intentionally overlapped their roles so that if their clients choose to purchase insurance or investment solutions that require a broker or dealer, those clients won't have to find an additional person to work with. Again, understanding the role of your professional will help you make your determination.

NARROWING THE FIELD
1. Decide on the Type of Professional with Whom You Want to Work. There are four basic kinds of financial professionals. Many professionals may play overlapping roles. It is important to know a professional's primary function, how they charge for their services and whether they are obligated to act in your best interest.

Registered representatives, better known as stockbrokers or bank / investment representatives, make their living by earning commissions on insurance solutions and investment services. Stockbrokers basically sell you things. The products from which they make the highest commission are sometimes the products that they recommend to their clients. If you want to make a simple transaction, such as buying or selling a particular stock, a registered representative can help you. Although registered representatives are licensed professionals, if you want to create a structured and planful approach to positioning your assets for retirement, you might want to consider continuing your search.

The term "planner" is often misused. It can refer to credible professionals that are CPAs, CFPs and ChFCs to your uncle's next-door neighbor who claims to have a lead on some undervalued stock about to be "discovered." A wide array of people may claim to be planners because there are no requirements to be a planner. The term financial planner, however, refers to someone who is properly registered as an investment advisor and serves as a fiduciary as described below.

Financial professionals are the diamonds in the rough. These Registered Investment Advisors are generally compensated on a fee basis. They do, however, often have licensure as stockbrokers or insurance agents, allowing them to earn commissions on certain transactions. More importantly, **financial professionals are financial fiduciaries, meaning they are required to make financial decisions in your best interest and reflecting your risk tolerance.** Investment Advisors are held to high ethical standards and are highly regarded in the financial industry. Financial professionals also often take a more comprehensive approach to asset management. These professionals are trained and credentialed to plan and coordinate their clients' assets in order to meet their goals or retirement and legacy planning. They are not focused on individual stocks, investments or markets. They look at the big picture, the whole enchilada.

Money managers are on par with financial professionals. However, they are often given explicit permission to make investment decisions without advanced approval by their clients.

Understanding who you are working with and what their title is the first step to planning your retirement. While each of the above-mentioned types of financial professionals can help you with aspects of your finances, it is **financial professionals** who have the most intimate role, the most objective investment strategies and the most unbiased mode of compensation for their services. A financial professional can also help you with the non-financial aspects of your legacy and can help you find ways to create a tax planning strategy to help you save money.

2. Be Objective. At the end of the day, you need to separate the weak from the strong. While you might want a strong personal rapport with your professional, or you may want to choose your professional for their personality and positive attitude, it is more important that you find someone who will give sage advice regarding achieving your retirement goals.

It can be helpful to use a process of elimination to narrow the field of potential professionals. Look into five or six potential leads and cross off your list the ones that don't meet your requirements until only one or two remain. Crosscheck your remaining choices against the list of things you need from a professional. Make sure they represent a firm that has the investment tools and solutions that you desire, and make sure they have experience in retirement planning. That is, after all, the main goal.

Don't be afraid to investigate each of your candidates. You'll want to ask the same questions and look for the same information from everyone you consider so you can then compare them and discern which is best for you. You'll want to take a look at the specific credentials of each professional, their experience and competence, their ethics and fiduciary status, their history and track record, and a list of the services that they offer. The professionals who meet all or most of your qualifications are the ones you will contact for an interview.

Potential professionals should meet your qualifications in the following categories:

- *Credentials:* Look at their experience, the quality of their education, any associations to which they belong and certifications they have earned. Someone who has continued their professional education through ongoing certifications will be more up-to-date on current financial practices compared to someone who got their degree 25 years ago and hasn't done a thing since.
- *Practices:* Look at the track record of your candidates, how they are compensated for their services, the reports and analysis they offer, and their value added services.
- *Services:* Your professional must meet your needs. If you are planning your retirement, you should work with someone who offers services that help you to that end. You want someone who can offer planning, advice on investment strategies, ways to calculate risk, advice on insurance and annuities solutions, and ways to manage your tax strategy.
- *Ethics:* You want to work with someone who is above board and does things the right way. Vet them by checking their compliance record, current licensing, fiduciary status and, yes, even their criminal record. You never know!

3. Ask for and Check References. Once you have selected two or three professionals that you want to meet, call or email them and ask for references. Every professional should be able to provide you with at least two or three names. In fact, they will probably be eager to share them with you. Most professionals rely on references for validation of their success, quality of services and likability. You should, however, take them with a grain of salt. You have no way to know whether or not references are a professional's friends or colleagues.

It is worth contacting references, however, to check for inconsistencies. Ask each reference the same set of questions to get the same basic information. How long have they been working with the professional? What kind of services have they used and were they happy with them? What type of financial planning did they use the professional for? Were they versed in the type of financial planning that you needed? You can also ask them direct questions to elicit candid responses. What was the full cost of the expenses that your professional charged you? Do the reports and statements you receive come from the same firm? Questions like these can help you get a sense of how well the reference knows their professional and whether or not they are a quality reference.

A good reference is a bit like icing on the cake. It's nice to have them, but nothing speaks louder than a good track record and quality experience. And remember that a good reference, while nice to hear, is relatively cheap. How many times have you heard someone on the golf course or at work telling you how great their stockbroker is? But how many times have you heard about the bad investments or losses they have experienced?

4. Use the Internet. As a final step before picking up the phone and calling your candidates, do some digging to discover if anyone on your list has a history of unlawful or unethical practices, or has been disciplined for any of their professional behavior or decisions. Don't worry, you don't have to hire a private investigator. You can easily find this information on the Financial Industry Regulatory Authority's (FINRA) online BrokerCheck tool: http://www.finra.org/Investors/ToolsCalculators/BrokerCheck/.

You should obviously explore the website of a potential professional and the website of the firm that they represent. The internet allows you to go beyond the online business card of a professional to gain access to information that they don't control. It may all be good information! Or a brief search of the internet could reveal a sketchy past. The best part is that the internet allows you to find helpful information in an anonymous fashion.

Start with Google (www.google.com) and search the name of a potential professional and their firm. Keep your eyes trained on third party sources such as articles, blog posts or news stories that mention the professional. You can also check a professional's compliance records online with the Financial Industry Regulatory Authority (FINRA) and the Securities and Exchange Commission (SEC). If you want to dig deeper, you can combine search terms like "scams," "lawsuits," "suspensions" and "fraud" with a professional's or firm's name to see what information arises. More likely than not, you won't find anything. But if you do, you'll be glad that you checked.

HOW TO INTERVIEW CANDIDATES

After vetting your candidates and narrowing down a list of professionals that you think might be a good fit for you, it's time to start interviewing.

When you meet in person with a professional, you want to take advantage of your time with them. The presentations and information that they share with you will be important to pay attention to, but you will also want to control some aspects of the interview. After a professional has told you what they want you to hear, it's time to ask your own questions to get the specific information you need to make your decision.

Make sure to prepare a list of questions and an informal agenda so that you can keep track of what you want to ask and what points you want the professional to touch on during the interview. Using the same questions and agenda will also allow you to more easily compare the professionals after you have interviewed them all. Remember that these interviews are just that, *interviews*. You are meeting with several professionals to determine with whom you want to work. Don't agree to anything or sign anything during an interview until after you have made your final decision.

It can also be helpful to put a time limit on your interviews and to meet the professionals at their offices. The time limit will keep things on track and will allow structured time for presentations and questions/discussion. By meeting them at their office, you can get a sense of the work environment, the staff culture and attitude, and how the firm does business. If you are unable to travel to a professional's office and must meet them at your home or office, make sure that your interviews are scheduled with plenty of time between so the professionals don't cross each other's paths.

You can use the following questions during an initial interview to get an understanding of how each professional does business and whether they are a good fit for you:

1. How do you charge for your services? How much do you charge? This information should be easy to find on their website, but if you don't see it, ask. Find out if they charge an initial planning fee, if they charge a percentage for assets under their management and if they make money by selling specific financial solutions or services. If so, you should follow up by asking how much the service costs. This will give you an idea of how they really make their money and if they have incentive to sell certain solutions over others. Make sure you understand exactly how you will be charged so there are no surprises down the road if you decide to work with this person.

2. What are your credentials, licenses, and certifications? There are Certified Financial Planners (CFPs), Chartered Financial Consultants (ChFCs), Investment Advisor Representatives, Certified Public Accountants (CPAs) and Personal Financial Specialists (PFSs). Whatever their credentials or titles, you want to be sure that the professional you work with is an expert in the field relevant to your circumstances. If you want someone to manage your money, you will most likely look for an Investment Advisor. Someone that works with an independent firm will likely have a team of CPAs, CFPs and other financial experts upon whom they can draw. If you like the professional you are meeting with and you think they might be a good fit, but they don't have the accounting experience you want them to have, ask about their firm and the resources available to them. If they work closely with CPAs that are experienced in your needs, it could be a good match.

3. What are the financial services that you and your firm provide? The question within the question here is, "Can you help me achieve my goals?" Some people can only provide you with investment advice, and others are tax consultants. You will likely want to work with someone that provides a complete suite of financial planning services and solutions that touch on retirement planning, insurance options, legacy and estate structuring, and tax planning. Whatever services they provide, make sure they meet your needs and your anticipated needs.

4. What kinds of clients do you work with the most? A lot of financial professionals work within a niche: retirement planning, risk assessment, life insurance, etc. Finding someone who works with other people that are in the same financial boat as you and who have similar goals can be an important way to make sure they understand your needs. While someone might be a crackerjack annuities cowboy, you might not be interested in that option. Ask follow-up questions that will really help you understand where their expertise lies and whether or not their experience lines up with your needs.

5. May I see a sample of one of your financial plans? You wouldn't buy a car without test-driving it, and you should not work with a professional without seeing a sample of how they do business. While there is no formal structure that a financial plan has to follow, the variation between professionals can help you find someone who "speaks your language." One professional may provide you with an in-depth analysis that relies heavily on info graphics and diagrams. Someone else may give you a seven-page review of your assets and general recommendations. By seeing a sample plan, you can narrow down who presents information in the way that you desire and in ways that you understand.

6. How do you approach investing? You may be entirely in the dark about how to approach your investments, or you might have some guiding principles. Either way, ask each candidate what their philosophy is. Some will resonate with you and some won't. A good professional who has a realistic approach to investing won't promise you the moon or tell you that they can make you a lot of money. Professionals who are successful at retirement planning and full service financial management will tell you that they will listen to your goals, risk tolerance and comfort level with different types of investment strategies. Working with someone that you trust is critical, and this question in particular can help you find out who you can and who you can't.

7. How do you remain in contact with your clients? Does your prospective professional hold annual, quarterly or monthly meetings? How often do *you* want to meet with your professional? Some people want to check in once a year, go over everything and make sure their ducks are all in a row. If any changes over the previous year or additions to their legacy planning strategy came up, they'll do it on that date. Other people want a monthly update to be more involved in the decision making process and to understand what's happening with their portfolio. You basically need to determine the right degree of involvement for both you and your financial professional. You'll also want to feel out how your professional communicates. Do you prefer phone calls or face-to-face meetings? Do you want your professional to explain things to you in detail or to summarize for you what decisions they've made? Is the professional willing to give you their direct phone number or their email address? More importantly, do you want that information and do you want to be able to contact them in those ways?

8. Are you my main contact, or do you work with a team? This is another way of finding out how involved with you your professional will be, and how often they will meet with you. It is also a way to discover how the firm they represent operates and manages their clients. Some professionals will answer their own phone, meet with you regularly and have your home phone number on speed dial. Others will meet with you once a year and have a partner or assistant check in with you every quarter to give you an update. Other companies take an entirely team-based approach whereby clients have a main contact but their portfolio is handled by a team of professionals that represent the firm. One way isn't better than another, but one way will be best for you. Find out how the professional you are interviewing operates before entering into an agreement.

9. How do you provide a unique experience for your clients? This is a polite way of asking, "Why should I work with you?" A professional should have a compelling answer to this question that connects with you. Their answer will likely touch on their investment philosophy, their communication style and their expertise. If you hear them describing strengths and philosophies that resonate with you, keep them on your list. Some professionals will tell you that they will make investments with your money that match your values, others will say they will maximize your returns and others will say they will protect your capital while structuring your assets for income. Whatever you're looking for in a professional, you will most likely find it in the answer to this question.

This last question you will want to ask *yourself* after you've met with someone who you are considering hiring:

10. Did they ask questions and show signs that they were interested in working with me? A professional who will structure your assets to reflect your risk tolerance and to position you for a comfortable retirement must be a good listener. You will want to pass by a professional who talks nonstop and tells you what to do without listening to what you want them to do. If you felt they listened well and understood your needs, and seemed interested and experienced in your situation, then they might be right for you.

THE IMPORTANCE OF INDEPENDENCE

Not all investment firms and financial professionals are created equal. The information in this book has systematically shown that leveraging investments for income and accumulation in today's market requires new ideas and modern planning. In short, you need innovative ideas to come up with the creative solutions that will provide you with the retirement that you want. Innovation thrives on independence. No matter how good a financial professional is, the firm that they represent needs to operate on principles that make sense in today's economy. Remember, advice about money has been around forever. Good advice, however, changes with the times.

Timing the market, relying on the sale of stocks for income and banking on high treasury and bond returns are not strategies. They aren't even realistic ways to make money or to generate income. Working with an independent agent can help you break free from the old ways of thinking and position you to create a realistic retirement plan.

Working with an independent professional who relies on fee-based income tied to the success of their performance will also give you greater peace of mind. When you do well, they do well, and that's the way it should be. Your independent financial professional will make sure that:
- Your assets are organized and structured to reflect your risk tolerance.
- Your assets will be available to you when you need them and in the way that you need them.
- You will have a lifetime income that will support your lifestyle through your retirement.
- You are handling your taxes as efficiently as possible.
- Your legacy is in order.
- Your Red Money is turned into Yellow Money, and is managed in your best interest.

What is your retirement dream? *Whatever it is, are you willing to let it remain a fantasy, or are you ready to make a plan? By working with an investment advisor who operates only in your best interests, you can create a strategic approach to your retirement that secures your lifestyle and provides you with income for the rest of your life. You need independent and objective advice to help build and cultivate trust between you and the person giving you the advice. Your advisor must put your needs and interests first and actively help you meet your goals and objectives and work with you on an on-going basis to make changes as needed.*

Now, ask yourself: Is your retirement built on hopes and dreams, or a solid, predictable plan?

IT'S WORTH IT!

Finding, interviewing and selecting a financial professional can seem like a daunting task. And honestly, it will take a good amount of work to narrow the field and find the one you want. In the end, it is worth the blood, sweat and tears. Your retirement, lifestyle, assets and legacy are on the line. The choices you make today will have lasting impacts on your life and the life of your loved ones. Working with someone you trust and know you can rely on to make decisions that will benefit you is invaluable. The work it takes to find them is something you will never regret.

Here is a recap of why working with a financial professional is the best retirement decision you can make:

CHAPTER 16 RECAP //

- If you feel you have more *Hope So* than *Know So* about your money and what your retirement is going to look like, working with a financial professional will give you clarity and confidence about what decisions are best for you.
- It is difficult for individual investors to not make emotional decisions about their investments. Financial professionals work with your risk tolerance, income needs and assets to find the most logical, efficient and beneficial way for you to structure your investments.
- As the DALBAR report showed, a majority of individual investors sell low when the market goes down and buy high when it goes back up. This is literally the exact opposite of what they should do to maximize their returns. Why? Emotions.
- A financial professional can help you change strategies when the market isn't going your way, but they won't abandon ship. They will stick to a planful approach. Your retirement isn't based on individual solutions or inves-

ments. It is based on a well-planned strategy that your financial professional is qualified to provide.
- Yellow Money is different from a mutual fund or a 401(k) because, while funds and 401(k)s are investment tools, they are not investment strategies. A 401(k) can be particularly misconceiving because your employer isn't truly structuring your investments inside the 401(k). They are simply providing you with a few options. The same goes for mutual funds. They are not truly managed by someone who is obligated to have your best interests and your risk tolerance in mind. In fact, the investment strategies of mutual funds change on a regular basis, and you might not know about it until you get an annual report a *month* later.
- The biggest difference between working with a financial professional to manage your funds, and buying a mutual fund is that, while a mutual fund buys 20 stocks and pegs its earnings on the overall performance of the portfolio, a financial professional works with you to create an overall financial strategy that meets your needs. It may or may not include mutual funds.
- As an individual investor, do you really have an overarching strategy for your financial portfolio? How did you come up with your selections? Do you know how they are individually managed? Do you know how to make changes to your portfolio that reflect your risk tolerance? Do you know what your risk tolerance is?
- Managed money has a specific criteria and a professional will fit that into your overall financial plan so that it works the way you want it to.
- Not all investment firms and financial professionals are created equal. Working with an independent professional will give you more options that are customizable to your life.

GLOSSARY*

ANNUAL RESET *(ANNUAL RATCHET, CLIQUET)* – Crediting methods measuring index movement over a one year period. Positive interest is calculated and credited at the end of each contract year and cannot be lost if the index subsequently declines. Say that the index increased from 100 to 110 in one year and the indexed annuity had an 80 percent participation rate. The insurance company would take the 10 percent gross index gain for the year (110-100/100), apply the participation rate (10 percent index gain x 80 percent rate) and credit 8 percent interest to the annuity. But, what if in the following year the index declined back to 100? The individual would keep the 8 percent interest earned and simply receive zero interest for the down year. An annual reset structure

---

* *"Glossary of Terms." FixedAnnuityFacts.com. NAFA, the National Association for Fixed Annuities, n.d. 12 Nov. 2013*

preserves credited gains and treats negative index periods as years with zero growth.

ANNUITANT – The person, usually the annuity owner, whose life expectancy is used to calculate the income payment amount on the annuity.

ANNUITY – An annuity is a contract issued by an insurance company that often serves as a type of savings plan used by individuals looking for long term growth and protection of assets that will likely be needed within retirement.

AVERAGING – Index values may either be measured from a start point to an end point (point-to-point) or values between the start point and end point may be averaged to determine an ending value. Index values may be averaged over the days, weeks, months or quarters of the period.

BENEFICIARY – A beneficiary is the person designated to receive payments due upon the death of the annuity owner or the annuitant themselves.

BONUS RATE – A bonus rate is the "extra" or "additional" interest paid during the first year (the initial guarantee period), typically used as an added incentive to get consumers to select their annuity policy over another.

CALL OPTION *(ALSO SEE PUT OPTION)* – Gives the holder the right to buy an underlying security or index at a specified price on or before a given date.

CAP – The maximum interest rate that will be credited to the annuity for the year or period. The cap usually refers to the maximum interest credited after applying the participation rate or yield spread. If the index methodology showed a 20 percent increase, the participation rate was 60 percent and the maximum interest cap was 10 percent, the contract would credit 10 percent interest. A few annuities use a maximum gain cap instead of a maximum interest cap with the participation rate or yield spread applied to the lesser of the gain or the cap. If the index methodology showed a 20 percent increase, the participation rate was 60 percent and the maximum gain cap was 10 percent, the contract would credit 6 percent interest.

COMPOUND INTEREST – Interest is earned on both the original principal and on previously earned interest. It is more favorable than simple interest. Suppose that your original principal was $1 and your interest rate was 10 percent for five years. With simple interest, your value is ($1 + $0.10 interest each year) = $1.50. With compound interest, your value is ($1 x 1.10 x 1.10 x 1.10 x 1.10 x 1.10) = $1.61. The advantage of compound interest over simple interest becomes greater as each subsequent period passes.

CREDITING METHOD *(ALSO SEE METHODOLOGY)* – The formula(s) used to determine the excess interest that is credited above the minimum interest guarantee.

DEATH BENEFITS – The payment the annuity owner's estate or beneficiaries will receive if he or she dies before the annuity matures. On most annuities, this is equal to the current account value. Some annuities offer an enhanced value at death via an optional rider that has a monthly or annual fee associated with it.

EXCESS INTEREST – Interest credited to the annuity contract above the minimum guaranteed interest rate. In an indexed annuity the excess interest is determined by applying a stated crediting method to a specific index or indices.

FIXED ANNUITY – A contract issued by an insurance company guaranteeing a minimum interest rate with the crediting of excess interest determined by the performance of the insurer's general account. Index annuities are fixed annuities.

FIXED DEFERRED ANNUITY – With fixed annuities, an insurance company offers a guaranteed interest rate plus safety of your principal and earnings ((subject to the claims-paying ability of the insurance company). Your interest rate will be reset periodically, based on economic and other factors, but is guaranteed to never fall below a certain rate.

FREE WITHDRAWALS – Withdrawals that are free of surrender charges.

INDEX – The underlying external benchmark upon which the crediting of excess interest is based, also a measure of the prices of a group of securities.

IRA *(INDIVIDUAL RETIREMENT ACCOUNT)* – An IRA is a tax-advantaged personal savings plan that lets an individual set aside money for retirement. All or part of the participant's contributions may be tax deductible, depending on the type of IRA chosen and the participant's personal financial circumstances. Distributions from many employer-sponsored retirement plans may be eligible to be rolled into an IRA to continue tax-deferred growth until the funds are needed. An annuity can be used as an IRA; that is, IRA funds can be used to purchase an annuity.

GLOSSARY

IRA ROLLOVER – IRA rollover is the phrase used when an individual who has a balance in an employer-sponsored retirement plan transfers that balance into an IRA. Such an exchange, when properly handled, is a tax-advantaged transaction.

LIQUIDITY – The ease with which an asset is convertible to cash. An asset with high liquidity provides flexibility, in that the owner can easily convert it to cash at any time, but it also tends to decrease profitability.

MARKET RISK – The risk of the market value of an asset fluctuating up or down over time. In a fixed or fixed indexed annuity, the original principal and credited interest are not subject to market risk. Even if the index declines, the annuity owner would receive no less than their original principal back if they decided to cash in the policy at the end of the surrender period. Unlike a security, indexed annuities guarantee the original premium and the premium is backed by, and is as safe as, the insurance company that issued it (subject to the claims-paying ability of the insurance company).

METHODOLOGY *(ALSO SEE CREDITING METHOD)* – The way that interest crediting is calculated. On fixed indexed annuities, there are a variety of different methods used to determine how index movement becomes interest credited.

MINIMUM GUARANTEED RETURN *(MINIMUM INTEREST RATE)* – Fixed indexed annuities typically provide a minimum guaranteed return over the life of the contract. At the time that the owner chooses to terminate the contract, the cash surrender value is compared to a second value calculated using the minimum guaranteed return and the higher of the two values is paid to the annuity owner.

OPTION – A contract which conveys to its holder the right, but not the obligation, to buy or sell something at a specified price on or before a given date. After this given date the option ceases to exist. Insurers typically buy options to provide for the excess interest potential. Options may be American style whereby they may be exercised at any time prior to the given date, or they may have to be exercised only during a specified window. Options that may only be exercised during a specified period are European-style options.

OPTION RISK – Most insurers create the potential for excess interest in an indexed annuity by buying options. Say that you could buy a share of stock for $50. If you bought the stock and it rose to $60 you could sell it and net a $10 profit. But, if the stock price fell to $40 you'd have a $10 loss. Instead of buying the actual stock, we could buy an option that gave us the right to buy the stock for $50 at any time over the next year. The cost of the option is $2. If the stock price rose to $60 we would exercise our option, buy the stock at $50 and make $10 (less the $2 cost of the option). If the price of the stock fell to $40, $30 or $10, we wouldn't use the option and it would expire. The loss is limited to $2—the cost of the option.

PARTICIPATION RATE – The percentage of positive index movement credited to the annuity. If the index methodology determined that the index increased 10 percent and the indexed annuity participated in 60 percent of the increase, it would be said that the contract has a 60 percent participation rate. Participation rates may also be expressed as asset fees or yield spreads.

POINT-TO-POINT – A crediting method measuring index movement from an absolute initial point to the absolute end point for a period. An index had a period starting value of 100 and a period ending value of 120. A point-to-point method would record a positive index movement of 20 [120-100] or a 20 percent positive movement [(120-100)/100]. Point-to-point usually refers to annual periods; however the phrase is also used instead of term end point to refer to multiple year periods.

PREMIUM BONUS – A premium bonus is additional money that is credited to the accumulation account of an annuity policy under certain conditions.

PUT OPTION *(ALSO SEE CALL OPTION)* – Gives the holder the right to sell an underlying security or index at a specified price on or before a given date.

QUALIFIED ANNUITIES *(QUALIFIED MONEY)* – Qualified annuities are annuities purchased for funding an IRA, 403(b) tax-deferred annuity or other type of retirement arrangements. An IRA or qualified retirement plan provides the tax deferral. An annuity contract should be used to fund an IRA or qualified retirement plan to benefit from an annuity's features other than tax deferral, including the safety features, lifetime income payout option and death benefit protection.

REQUIRED MINIMUM DISTRIBUTION *(RMD)* – The amount of money that Traditional, SEP and SIMPLE IRA owners and qualified plan participants must begin distributing from their retirement accounts by April 1 following the year they reach age 70.5. RMD amounts must then be distributed each subsequent year.

RETURN FLOOR – Another way of saying minimum guaranteed return.

ROTH IRA – Like other IRA accounts, the Roth IRA is simply a holding account that manages your stocks, bonds, annuities, mutual funds and CD's. However, future withdrawals (including earnings and interest) are typically tax-advantaged once the account has been open for five years and the account holder is age 59.5.

RULE OF 72 – Tells you approximately how many years it takes a sum to double at a given rate. It's handy to be able to figure out, without using a calculator, that when you're earning a 6 percent return, for example, by dividing 6 percent into 72, you'll find that it takes 12 years for money to double. Conversely, if you know it took a sum twelve years to double you could divide 12 into 72 to determine the annual return (6 percent).

SIMPLE INTEREST *(ALSO SEE COMPOUND INTEREST)* – Interest is only earned on the principal balance.

SPLIT ANNUITY – A split annuity is the term given to an effective strategy that utilizes two or more different annuity products—one designed to generate monthly income and the other to restore the original starting principal over a set period of time.

STANDARD & POOR'S 500 *(S&P 500)* – The most widely used external index by fixed indexed annuities. Its objective is to be a benchmark to measure and report overall U.S. stock market performance. It includes a representative sample of 500 common stocks from companies trading on the New York Stock Exchange, American Stock Exchange, and NASDAQ National Market System. The index represents the price or market value of the underlying stocks and does not include the value of reinvested dividends of the underlying stocks.

GLOSSARY

STOCK MARKET INDEX – A report created from a type of statistical measurement that shows up or down changes in a specific financial market, usually expressed as points and as a percentage, , in a number of related markets, or in an economy as a whole (i.e. S&P 500 or New York Stock Exchange).

SURRENDER CHARGE – A charge imposed for withdrawing funds or terminating an annuity contract prematurely. There is no industry standard for surrender charges, that is, each annuity product has its own unique surrender charge schedule. The charge is usually expressed as a percentage of the amount withdrawn prematurely from the contract. The percentage tends to decline over time, ultimately becoming zero.

TRADITIONAL IRA – See IRA (Individual Retirement Account)

TERM END POINT – Crediting methods measuring index movements over a greater timeframe than a year or two. The opposite of an annual reset method. Also referred to as a term point-to-point method. Say that the index value was at 100 on the first day of the period. If the calculated index value was at 150 at the end of the period the positive index movement would be 50 percent (150-100/100). The company would credit a percentage of this movement as excess interest. Index movement is calculated and interest credited at the end of the term and interim movements during the period are ignored.

TERM HIGH POINT *(HIGH WATER MARK)* – A type of term end point structure that uses the highest anniversary index level as the end point. Say that the index value was at 100 on the first day of the period, reached a value of 160 at the end of a contract year during the period, and ended the period at 150. A term high point method would use the 160 value—the highest contract anniversary point reached during the period, as the end point and the gross index gain would be 60 percent (160-100/100). The company would then apply a participation rate to the gain.

TERM YIELD SPREAD – A type of term end point structure which calculates the total index gain for a period, computes the annual compound rate of return deducts a yield spread from the annual rate of return and then recalculates the total index gain for the period based on the net annual rate. Say that an index increased from 100 to 200 by the end of a nine year period. This is the equivalent of an 8 percent compound annual interest rate. If the annuity had a 2 percent term yield spread this would be deducted from the annual interest rate (8 percent-2 percent) and the net rate would be credited to the contract (6 percent) for each of the nine years. Total index gain may also be computed by using the highest anniversary index level as the end point.

VARIABLE ANNUITY – A contract issued by an insurance company offering separate accounts invested in a wide variety of stocks and/or bonds. The investment risk is borne by the annuity owner. Variable annuities are considered securities and require appropriate securities registration.

1035 EXCHANGE – The 1035 exchange refers to the section of tax code that allows annuity owners the flexibility to exchange one annuity for another without incurring any immediate tax liabilities. This action is most often utilized when an annuity holder decides they want to upgrade an annuity to a more favorable one, but they do not want to activate unnecessary tax liabilities that would typically be encountered when surrendering an existing annuity contract.

401(K) ROLLOVER – See <u>IRA Rollover</u>